MW01294623

COMING BACK

MATTHEW 6:34

JEFFERY L. COFFEY

authorHOUSE®

AuthorHouse™
1663 Liberty Drive
Bloomington, IN 47403
www.authorhouse.com
Phone: 1-800-839-8640

First published by AuthorHouse 8/13/2010

ISBN: 978-1-4520-1384-8 (e)
ISBN: 978-1-4520-1382-4 (sc)
ISBN: 978-1-4520-1383-1 (hc)

Library of Congress Control Number: 2010910736

Printed in the United States of America

This book is printed on acid-free paper.

Foreword By Coach Bill Payne

Caldwell Community College Head Basketball Coach

The first time I heard the name Jeff Coffey, I received an email from him. Jeff's email began "This may be the strangest email you have ever received". At the age of 44 he was inquiring about playing college basketball. I was in the process of recruiting his son Jeremy. I invited Jeff and Jeremy to a summer workout. He came to one of our tryouts and we talked a long time about basketball and college. During the conversation I found out that Jeff had already played at Caldwell Community College right out of high school in 1977. He said he had been playing most of the time since he left college. Jeff mentioned that he might be interested in playing his second year at Caldwell Community College and Technical Institute. He then came to several workouts and I realized he could be a very valuable asset to our team in more ways than just a player. Jeff had already coached at the community college level and was familiar with what was needed to be successful.

At our first regular practice, we were doing conditioning drills. I had them doing plyometrics by jumping up on the first bleacher from the floor and as Jeff was doing this he missed the bleacher and slid off the step and gouged both of his shins deeply. For most players this injury would have shelved them for several days but not

Jeff. He was ready to scrimmage five minutes later. As the season began, Jeff earned his place in our rotation. He would come into the game and do several things for us. If we needed an opposing post player stopped, that is what he did. If we needed some rebounds or points, that's what he did. He would also calm the team when they needed someone to settle them down. His job was to be a coach on the floor and on the bench. All of our players really respected Jeff for what he was doing, including his son Jeremy.I never took it easy on him he practiced just as hard as every other player. Remember he was working full time with his business, was a full time father, as well as working as a full time student. Years later I look back and still find that what he accomplished was absolutely amazing!!

Coach William Payne

"I admire your courage and understand the strength it took to return to the court."

Conner Shell   Director of Development   ESPN Entertainment

INTRODUCTION

I have enjoyed writing books and poetry since the age of twelve. The first book I penned (well, actually penciled) was written on notebook paper in cursive writing. That was when we were actually taught how to write in cursive and used it as a means of communication. My first book was a fictional work titled *The Ocean House*. It was a mystery with a dash of horror added. It was about friends meeting for a weeklong vacation on the coast of Massachusetts. I have no idea where that manuscript is today. My second book was also handwritten at the age of fourteen. The title was *Come Back*. It was a fictional sports story. The main character was cut from his high school junior varsity basketball team as a freshman. The players and his friends made fun of him. Soon after, he and his family moved across the state, several hundred miles away. Three years later, through his hard work and determination, he became a great player. In the final chapter, he faced his old high school and former friends for the state championship. Of course, his team won and he had the last laugh. My third book, *Fast Food to Fast Breaks,* was never completed. *Coming Back* will be my first published work.

I am surprised I am finally having a book published. I'm sure my family, friends, and former teachers will be surprised also. To understand why everyone will be so surprised, you need to have an understanding of my background—where I came from. I was born in 1959 in Lincolnton, North Carolina. My grandparents and parents were devout Christians. They made sure that all of the children and grandchildren knew right from wrong. They also believed that every word in the Bible was fact, and that's what we were taught. I still believe and teach that the world was made in seven days. I believe in Adam and Eve and Noah's Ark. I have no reason not to believe.

Besides being devout Christians, they were also hard workers. My family all worked in cotton mills during some point in their adult lives. They all worked hard and all strived for a better life. Through their desire and work ethic, they were able to advance to better situations and were able to provide better lives for themselves and their families. Despite the long hours and hard work, they were always happy and content. From watching them I knew that quitting school or not working would never be options in my life. Each one of my parents and grandparents helped me obtain summer jobs at some point. One summer I worked at the J. P. Stevens cotton mill in Boger City. Yes, even I experienced firsthand the hard work of the cotton mill. I think they got me those jobs to teach me lessons in life. Number one: you do not want to spend your life working in a cotton mill. Lesson learned. The same Christian values, work ethics, and determination that they taught me guided me through all the years of my basketball, business, and personal comebacks that life has required. It was also these same attributes that provided me with the determination to complete the writing of *Coming Back*.

I decided to write *Coming Back* in June 2004. I was attempting to come back to Caldwell Community College in Hudson, North

Carolina, and play college basketball at the age of forty-five. I started a diary that summer with the intentions of writing a book about my experiences during the season. I thought it was a unique story for several reasons. First was the fact that I was forty-five years of age and would become the oldest college basketball player in history. Second, I was playing for a team that I had a 7–0 coaching record against as a rival years earlier. Finally, there was the fact that I played on the same team as my son Jeremy.

As the first chapter evolved, *Coming Back* became much more than just a story about my basketball comeback. It became a story of lessons I have learned and comebacks made in my life, my family's life, and the life of our great nation. The deeper I dug, the more I realized that my whole life has been marked by a series of comebacks. Then I thought about the fact that many people's lives have progressed in the same way.

I hope that my comebacks will provide others with hope, strength, inspiration, and determination while they are making their own comebacks. There are several stories contained in my comebacks that were hard for me to share. I did so after much prayer, asking God what good my stories could do for others. Hopefully there are stories that will inspire you, make you laugh, and make you cry, and others that will make you say "wow." After five years of writing and many months of AnnaMarie telling me to "please finish the book," my work is done.

The fact that you are reading this book is amazing to me and has made it worth the time and effort to write. If *Coming Back* inspires, motivates, eases pain, or gives hope or strength to even one person, my job is done and *Coming Back* has been a successful venture. One more comeback in my life is now complete.

Therefore do not worry about tomorrow, for tomorrow will worry about itself. Each day has enough trouble of its own. Matthew 6:34

Comeback: a noun meaning a return to a higher rank, popularity, position, prosperity, or better situation. The word has many different meanings, and a different meaning to every individual, family, business, and even our own country. The term is used in all facets of life, including athletics, business, news events, and our personal lives. Take a look in the mirror. Now take a look at any of your photos that include you, your family, friends, co-workers, and even strangers. The person that you see in the mirror and everyone in those photos has faced major setbacks in their lives that they have had to come back from. Everyone in every phase of life experiences setbacks, and comebacks. Some are minor, but be assured some are or will be major. During every stage of our childhood, teen years, young adult life, the middle ages, and through the golden years, we all experience ups and downs, highs and lows. How we come back from the downs and the lows helps determine the quality of our life, our happiness, and the type of influence we'll have on our family and all of those around us. Our relationship with God, our marital relationship, business relationships, child rearing, and the pursuit of life's individual goals all require the ability to come back

1

from the curve balls and adversities that life throws at each and every one of us.

Comebacks are not limited to each of us as individuals. Entire countries are forced to make comebacks. They all face adversities and events that they have to come back from. In the case of countries, these comebacks may take centuries, as was the case of Rome's comeback from its great fall on September 4, 476 AD. In some cases the time might be limited to decades, such as the United States' recovery from the Great Depression, which began in 1929. While countries can and do come back from adversity, the most important comebacks and the ones that matter most are the ones that we make in our own lives.

These comebacks depend upon the individual alone. They do not take centuries or decades. Most of us face comebacks on a daily, weekly, monthly, and yearly basis. We must recognize that these comebacks not only serve to make each of us stronger in character, but they also prepare us for the next test that we will face. There will be more. A lifetime full, to be exact. God will, without fail, help us through these trying times. The sooner we learn to depend on Him in the good times, as well as these times of trial and tribulation, the sooner we are able to understand that these tests, trials, and curve balls in life do serve a purpose. They are meaningful, insightful, and are beneficial in the circle, or as I call it, the circus of life.

There are many people who do not have the faith and strength to come back from life's trials. Thus we have suicide, an alarming increase in our crime rate, and more homeless people than at any other time in history. During my own learning process of these lessons in life, I, like all humans, have experienced happiness, sadness, jubilation, devastation, and every emotion in between.

While preparing for my latest comeback, I began seeing my entire life as a long series of individual setbacks and comebacks. I started observing my family, friends, celebrities, and even strangers. I learned that everyone has problems they must come back from. It's not just you and me. I had a stunning revelation ... life is not ever going to be perfect. No, not ever, so enjoy every single day for what it is, a gift from God

At the same time, I started taking a look at the people and the nation around me. That's when I realized that not only is every individual on a comeback trail, but also the United States faces a comeback trail of its own in order to survive. There is something to be said for the good old days. Our country needs to return to the days of love, morality, fairness, justice, charity, good business sense, and logical decision making. There can be, and needs to be, a coming back of the old American way of life, with close-knit communities. Communities made up of individuals helping one another instead of hurting, cheating, robbing, and killing one another. As a nation, if we continue on our current path, our country will not come back, and will eventually implode. The implosion will be due to a lack of love, morals, common sense, and a lack of good work ethics

As far back as November 21, 1864, Abraham Lincoln said, "I see in the near future a crisis approaching that unnerves me and causes me to tremble for the safety of my country ... corporations have been enthroned and an era of corruption in high places will follow, and the money power of the country will endeavor to prolong its rein by working on the prejudices of the people until all wealth is aggregated in a few hands and the Republic is destroyed."

This is exactly where our country stands 146 years later. Our lives have become too fast paced, and we have become too intelligent and advanced for our own good or for the good of our nation as a whole. Many crimes are committed against individuals and families due to the improper use of something as simple as the Internet. From embezzlement, kidnapping, theft, rape, and child molestation, to the ultimate crime of murder, the Internet has been used to commit each of these crimes many times over. Was it really that bad having to look a word up in the dictionary or learning history from an encyclopedia? I'm unaware of any crimes committed because of *Webster's Dictionary* or the *World Book Encyclopedia*.

Technology's negative effect goes much further than just the Internet. Most of the children and teens in the United States spend far too much time on the computer, playing video games, listening to iPods, talking on cell phones, and watching television. That's probably the only issue that President Obama and I have agreed on since he took office. At his commencement speech at Hampton University in May 2010 he stated "And with iPods and iPads, and Xboxes and PlayStations—none of which I know how to work—information becomes a distraction, a diversion, a form of entertainment, rather than a tool of empowerment, rather than the means of emancipation. So all of this is not only putting pressure on you; it's putting new pressure on our country and on our democracy."

It's our responsibility as educators, parents, and grandparents to make sure the next generation has other interests that will be healthy and lead not only to building their minds, bodies, and self-esteem, but will also provide our country with the leadership it requires to come back and be a successful nation once again. The current generation will be the generation that initiates our country's comeback, if a comeback is to be generated.

In everyone's life there has to be a purpose and a goal for each stage of that life. Without goals a person's life is like going on a long trip with no map and no directions, no destination. You'll get lost! After many years I realized that I used basketball as my outlet, my character builder, and it played a large part in forming me into the person I am today. For others it might be art, music, photography, religion, or any other interest, but everyone has something in life that makes him or her who he or she is and helps to develop him or her into who he or she will become. When I look back on my life, there are certain events that are fresh in my memories of setbacks and comebacks. There are events that involve not only the early years of my life, but also comebacks that involve myself, my children, and others around me.

In January 2005, a much prayed for, much anticipated comeback became another memory that I will always cherish. I returned to Caldwell Community College after a twenty-eight-year absence, the same college where in 1977, my college education and college basketball career was launched. When I returned in 2005, I wanted to finish something I had started but had quit, and had dreamed of for many years, a college basketball career. It took the comeback of a lifetime to recover from two heart attacks in order to play competitive college basketball at the age of forty-six.

I started at Caldwell Community College in Hudson, NC, as an All American basketball player in September 1977. When I returned in 2005, I became "Grandpa," the oldest college basketball player in history. I was fortunate enough to play on the same nationally ranked NJCAA (National Junior College Athletic Association) basketball team as my son Jeremy. It was also for the same college team that I had coached against ten years prior.

During this comeback attempt, I became even more aware that everyone has good times and bad times. God does not create bad instances or events that happen in our lives. He has given us free will, the privilege to choose and make decisions. While God is watching over us, Satan is testing us as he attempts to build his own army all over the world. Some people choose God's way while others choose Satan's evil ways. That choice does not determine a person's wealth or happiness on earth. More importantly, it determines where each and every one of us will spend eternity.

This belief helps me answer the oft asked question, "Why do bad things happen to good people and good things happen to bad people?" In January 2010 an earthquake killed over one hundred thousand people in Haiti. Some media personalities and different religious activists speculated that God had brought this earthquake upon Haiti to punish the people there because of their religious beliefs. Guess what? That is not what happened! The plates in the earth caused the ground to shift and caused the earthquake. Just as the earthquake was not sent from God, serial killers, murderers, and Hurricane Katrina were not God's will. God was not mad at the city of New Orleans. In the book of Genesis, God knew that Cain killed Abel, but that was not God's will. That was Cain acting on his own, using his free will to complete the act. Every single person has the free will to live his life as he desires and to act as he desires, good or bad. Every person fights his or her own battles. Sometimes there are victories; sometimes we face defeat.

Actors, professional athletes, business managers, famous singers, and even a native living alone on an island are all on their own comeback voyages in one form or another. Problems and issues can range from hunger, unemployment, addiction, crime, finances, family problems, or may be a combination of many issues. My dear wife Anna Marie believes that if a group of people carrying their own troubles in a sack sat down together and shared their troubles, each and every person there would be happy to get up, take their own sack of troubles, and go back home. The moral of her story is that everyone's life could be worse than it is.

I began writing my third book in 1993. The title was *Fast Food to Fast Breaks*. The book was based on my rise from being a fast-food restaurant manager to a successful NJCAA basketball coach in a short five-year span. The successes I experienced led me to hope I would soon realize my dream of becoming a NCAA basketball coach. After completing the first three chapters of the book, my career and life experienced a catastrophic turn of events. I went from being a college basketball coach with a promising future to being unemployed, through no fault of my own. I felt like all of the work, effort, and time I spent preparing myself to coach at the NCAA level had been a waste of time. It was at that time that I realized, sometimes things just happen, and we have to work to make the best of it. If we cry and dwell on every issue that arises, or every curve ball that life throws at us, we will never find the time to enjoy life as God intended us to. The good times and the bad times begin at an early age, and we are faced with them throughout our entire life.

From childhood on, my life has been filled with good times and bad times, setbacks and comebacks. If I could, I would not change a thing, as each individual setback and ensuing comeback has made me stronger and helped me to realize the importance of faith and determination, and has eventually led to success. These unique situations also provided me with the strength necessary for my latest comeback attempt. During my attempt to return to play college basketball, there were many comebacks within the initial comeback. This comeback trail was not an easy one, as it was filled with many bumps along the route to success. I am fortunate that from my childhood on I was faced with obstacles and situations that had to be overcome in order to gain the strength, knowledge, and faith that were required to return to play college basketball at the age of forty-six.

As the time approached for my comeback at Caldwell Community College, I realized my life completed a full circle. There were many comebacks within that circle, and I began examining how I turned to God in each and every situation for strength and comfort. I believe that the foundation for my life, and my ability to come back, was built within the first eighteen years of my life. This comes as no surprise, because one common thread that binds many scientific studies is the fact that a person's adolescent years play a large role in molding who that person will become. This includes religious beliefs, morals, and work ethics. These years are crucial in developing the faith and the strength that is required to come back from issues throughout our lives, while still being happy and productive members of society. I was fortunate to have parents, grandparents, and great-grandparents who taught me right from wrong on a daily basis, and taught me the value of hard work.

I examined my life, my own comebacks, and the comebacks of those around me, arriving at the realization that a small thing like the sport of basketball played a great role in making me who I am today. The work ethic that brought me basketball success taught me that almost anything can be accomplished if a person is willing to work hard to achieve a goal. The problems and issues, wins and losses, that were a part of my basketball career were all beneficial in making me a stronger person, and prepared me for my future endeavors. I dug deep into my memory bank to trace how I became the person I am today, and how my setbacks and ensuing comebacks molded me and gave me the strength to become "Grandpa," the oldest college basketball player in history.

The Coffey family, like everyone in your pictures, everyone in this picture has faced many setbacks and ensuing comebacks, with many more to come.

The Lord directs our steps, so why try to understand everything along the way? Proverbs 20:24

From the time I was five years old, my parents and grandparents made sure that my brother Kevin and I had a basketball goal in our backyard. At five years of age I was fascinated by the game of basketball and the strategies involved. It still amazes me how I was able to understand and comprehend the game at that early age. I enjoyed watching, learning, and playing basketball. I stayed outside shooting baskets until well after dark, when my mom forced me to come inside. Practicing was not something I had to do; it was sheer enjoyment for me. I shot baskets in the rain, snow, and in the midday heat of the summer days. I did not think about getting sunburned, catching a cold, getting too tired, or any of the other excuses I hear from many of today's youth. My entire family participated. My grandmother Mamma Davis, my dad, and my mom all came outside and shot baskets with my brother Kevin and me. These are the same people who helped mold me in many other ways, and provided me with many memories that I still cherish today.

I played basketball for many hours alone because there were not any organized youth leagues or AAU basketball teams. My first true basketball "game" experience came when I was ten years old and in the fourth grade. I attended Asbury Elementary School in Lincolnton, NC. There were four fourth grade classes. The teachers decided to have a classroom basketball tournament for the boys and a softball tournament for the girls. These tournaments were held on field day, in my opinion the second best school day of the year! (The last day of school was always number one in my book.) I thought that the basketball tournament was just about the greatest thing that had ever happened to me. I was so excited, I tortured my coach, who taught fifth grade, by calling him every day at his house with strategies, ideas, and tips on how we could win. I'm sure now that he didn't understand a thing I was saying.

I was in Mrs. Carpenter's class. The players' mothers made uniforms out of white T-shirts by writing "Carpenter's Crew" on the front and numbers on the back. The games were played on an outdoor asphalt court. My class won both games 8–6 and 8–2 to claim the Asbury School fourth grade class championship. I made every point that our team scored! It helped that I was a foot taller than everyone else. That one-day field day event increased my desire to become a better basketball player and learn how to reach goals through hard work.

The following year I was invited to the Iron Station basketball tryouts. This was a team made up of fifth through eighth grade boys that assembled to play in the Lincolnton Optimist Tournament. The tournament was the biggest junior high school tournament of the year. It was the only time that the "city boys" squared off against the "country boys." The city champions could conceivably end up meeting the county champions. That was the matchup the players and fans longed for. I practiced for months and believed that I was going to attend the Iron Station tryouts, be selected for the team, and be the only fifth grader to actually ever play in the Optimist

Tournament. At the same time, my friends and family tried to tell me there was no way I could make the team. Being hardheaded, I still thought that I'd make the cut, until I walked into the gym.

A big factor that I had failed to calculate in my great plan was the difference in the size and strength of an eighth grader and a fifth grader. I walked into the gym and was the shortest player there. I was five feet seven inches tall; tall for an eleven-year-old, but not tall for a fourteen-year-old. I was the only fifth or sixth grader in the gym, and there was a good reason for that. I wished that I had stayed home, and all I wanted to do was to get the tryout over with and get out of there. I played well for a fifth grader, but not good enough to make the team. I was embarrassed the following week at school when all the kids, including my friends, enjoyed telling me "I told you so." It was not until many years later that I realized I had learned a good lesson, and the experience had made me a stronger, more determined person.

Despite the disappointment of not being selected for the Iron Station basketball team, I had no thoughts of quitting the sport. I did not see my being cut from the team as a failure; I saw it as a fact of age difference, size difference, and a need to work even harder to get better. I spent the following six months practicing basketball four to six hours every weekday, and ten to twelve hours a day on the weekends. I practiced so much that the ends of my fingers split open and bled. The sand of a dirt court eats through the skin until there is no skin left. I learned quickly that I could not shoot the basketball with Band-Aids on my fingertips, so I accepted the pain and played on.

That same year my parents bought me a guitar for Christmas. They also bought albums by Johnny Cash, Charlie Pride, and Jerry Lee Lewis. The first two weeks after Christmas, I played basketball, played guitar, played more basketball, then played more guitar. At the beginning of the third month, in order to save my fingertips for basketball, I gave up the guitar. Playing a guitar takes as severe a toll on fingertips as a dirt basketball court does. I also realized I was a much better basketball player than guitar player. When I wasn't playing basketball, I was listening to Davidson Wildcat basketball on the radio or watching the Carolina Tar Heels on television.

During this same time, a certain experience caused me to realize that I spent most of my free time playing basketball and that I had very few other interests. My brother Kevin and I bought model cars on the same day. We started to work on them as soon as we returned home from the Rose's dime store. Within two hours my model was finished and I was outside playing basketball again. Two days later my brother's model was finished. You could tell the difference. His model looked like it had been driven off the showroom floor, while my model looked like it should be sitting in a junkyard. I just knew I would rather be shooting baskets than sitting in the house!

The following year I attended Central Junior High School in Lincolnton, NC. I entered the sixth grade with every intention of playing in the Lincolnton Optimist Tournament. I knew that I was too young to play on the school team, but the Optimist Tournament was different. I thought I could make the team if any additional players were added. February 1971 rolled around, and our junior high team completed a championship regular season. When the season ended, I knew there would be roster changes due to the age limits that the Optimist Tournament adhered to. My brother Kevin was on the Central team, and I wanted to be on it too. I met with Central's basketball coach, Mr. Shelton. He was a large man with a deep voice and everyone was afraid of him. His size and voice were not what everyone feared; it was his paddle. I guess our country no longer believes paddling is a good thing, so they don't allow it anymore, but it sure kept us on the straight and narrow path!

Coach Shelton ignored me as he walked into the gym. I then waited through practice. I met him in the gym after practice and asked him if I could try out for the tournament team. He smiled, looked down at me, and explained that no sixth grader had ever played in the Lincolnton Optimist Tournament. He told me that I needed to continue to work hard and try out for the school team the following season. This was disappointing news to me, and I asked God why He had allowed this to happen to me. At the time, I did not realize that this was not God's way of punishing me. It all had to do with Coach Shelton's own free will and his decision-making process. He had the free will to make and enforce his own rules. Many years later I understood and respected Mr. Shelton and his decisions, as they were the correct ones. I think he sensed that my opportunity would one day come, but that season belonged to the older players who had worked to get there. I became even more determined that when my opportunity did come, I would be able to seize it!

My first basketball goal at age five. I already loved the game, and flying kites.

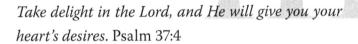

Take delight in the Lord, and He will give you your heart's desires. Psalm 37:4

The following summer, Mamma and Granddaddy Davis paid for my brother Kevin and me to attend Ashbrook High School's basketball school, conducted by Coach Larry Rhodes. Coach Rhodes was the first real coach that I ever played for. I was excited about going to a weeklong basketball school, and the camp turned out to be even better than I imagined. Five days of basketball drills, instructions, games, films, and two McDonald's cheeseburgers for lunch. Some people would say "no way," but I was in basketball heaven!

I entered the seventh grade at Central Junior High in August 1971 determined to make the eighth grade team. I knew Mr. Shelton would have to be impressed, or the spot would go to an older eighth grader. I felt I had a good chance, because I played basketball games during physical education class with the eighth grade players and could compete on an even basis with the projected starters. After a week of tryouts, the team was announced. On that Monday I went to school an hour early and ran straight to the gym door to see the team list. I started reading from the top of the list: Chris Alexander, Mike Beal, Greg Bradley. I was sweating as I neared the bottom of the list.

The next to last name was Jeff Coffey. I was one of two seventh graders that made the team!

I was happy to be on the team, but there was just one catch. Seventh graders did not get uniforms. We practiced every day and dressed for every game in a white T-shirt and white shorts. Since we were the Central Patriots and the other players wore red, white, and blue uniforms, those white uniforms stuck out, to say the least. If an eighth grade teammate was out sick or absent on a game day, Chuck Hartzog (the other seventh grader) and I flipped a coin to see who would wear the vacant red, white, and blue uniform. It did not matter that we practiced as hard or played as much as anyone else. We were seventh graders, so we wore the white uniforms.

The 1971–72 regular season ended, and I could hardly wait for the Lincolnton Optimist Tournament to begin. We lost several players due to the tournament's age restrictions. I was not only going to have a team uniform, but maybe even get more playing time in the "Biggest Show On Earth." Well ,that's what it was to me at that time. Our Central team won our first two games to advance to the championship game against the top city school, S. Ray Lowder. I played twelve or thirteen minutes each night. On the Saturday we were to play for the championship, our starting center contracted the flu and was unable to play. While I was sorry my teammate was sick, I was happy for the opportunity to play more minutes. I was a seventh grader starting in the eighth-grade tournament that I had dreamed about for the previous three years! To this day, I remember thanking God for letting me finally reach my goal. I learned that even if things did not go my way, I could keep coming back until the desired result was achieved. This is a lesson I have carried throughout my athletic, professional, and personal life.

The evening of the championship game, the Lincolnton High School gym was sold out. I had never seen so many people at a local game before. I was nervous because it was the biggest game of my life. I responded with eight points and ten rebounds in a 38–36 overtime loss. The loss stung, and was very disappointing, but I knew that I accomplished something special that evening. That performance gave me the desire to continue to work hard, come back better, and win the Optimist Tournament title in 1973.

The following month I dedicated my life to Christ at Riverview Baptist Church in Lincolnton. It seemed fitting that this was the place I accepted the Lord. My great-grandfather donated the land for the first church built there. My great-grandparents, grandparents, aunts, uncles, and father were lifelong members. I remember that one Sunday morning as the most important day of my life. From that point on, I always had a friend that gave me strength and faith to come back from whatever befell me.

The following summer, before my eighth grade year, I once again attended the Ashbrook High School basketball school and tried to learn everything I could from Coach Rhodes. After the camp, I spent the entire summer, eight to ten hours per day, practicing the drills I had learned. In my mind the Optimist Tournament comeback was not yet complete. I looked forward to my eighth grade year with a lot of anticipation. My anticipation was not because of school. At that point I thought I went to school just to play basketball. I grew two inches over the summer, and was now six feet and two inches tall.

The season started out just as I hoped. Our team was having

a good year, and I was having a record-breaking season. In early January our scorekeeper and my good friend Steve Harrill informed me that I needed sixty-two points to break the school's all-time scoring record. I knew that with seven games to go, it was a cinch. In our next game we faced Love Memorial Junior High. I scored thirty-three points, breaking the Central Junior High School's record for the most points scored in one game. I was only twenty-nine points away from the school's scoring record. I thanked God every day, and appreciated the gifts He had bestowed upon me. I was setting new school records, getting my name in the local paper, and just enjoying my life. The best part of all was that the highly anticipated Lincolnton Optimist Tournament was only a month away. I was determined to leading Central Junior High to its first ever Lincoln Optimist Championship title.

The week following the Love Memorial game, I was practicing and jammed my hand against the rim of the basketball hoop. I heard two loud "pops." An intense pain shot through my hand and arm. Later that afternoon my mother took me to see an orthopedic doctor. After examining my hand and taking X-rays, he left the room. Ten minutes later he returned to the examination room, unaware of the implications of the news he was about to deliver.

"Well, you have a broken middle finger and a severely sprained index finger. I am putting a cast on your hand and we'll check it again in four weeks."

I would be unable to play basketball again until March. Playing would risk further damage and possibly lead to surgery. Tears welled up in my eyes, and I cried on the trip home. That was one of the lowest points in my life. My world went from everything I had ever hoped for as a basketball player, to not breaking the school scoring record, possibly no county title, and, worst of all, no Lincolnton Optimist Tournament. I had waited four long years for this opportunity, but now the dream appeared to be just that ... only a dream.

I still went to practice the next day and ran sprints, dribbled with my left hand, even started shooting with my left hand. I shot jump shots, hook shots, layups, all left-handed. At the time I thought that God was punishing me for being mean to my sister Sue Ellen, or for looking at a friend's *Playboy* magazine. I did not realize that God was actually bestowing a gift upon me that I would benefit from for my entire basketball career.

Our team won four of five contests in my absence, and entered the final week of the Lincoln County Junior High Championship season with a one-game advantage in the standings over rival Rock Springs. We faced Rock Springs in the last game of the regular season. I begged my doctor, my parents, and anyone else who would listen, to please let me play in this last game, which would determine the county championship. The answer was *no!* During the game I sat in the stands at Rock Springs School and watched as we fell behind by sixteen points at halftime. I begged my mom, once again, to let me dress out for the second half. Once again the answer was *no!* My beloved Patriots lost by twenty points to Rock Springs, so we shared the county title with them.

The following week I went to the doctor. My cast was removed, replaced by a splint. I continued to work with the team and could use my right hand to some degree. Three days before the Optimist Tournament, I prayed many times and asked, actually begged, God to heal me so that I could play. It's funny the small things we pray for as children and teens that seem so big at the time, but appear so minute when we're adults. I called the doctor at his office without my parent's knowledge. I explained the situation to him and told him how much this tournament meant to me. He said that he could not recommend that I play, but that it was my decision. I approached my parents with this information. Of course, I sugar-coated it a little ... Well, a lot! My dad said to "tape it up" and play. To my surprise, my mom agreed. I knew this was God answering my prayers, because my mom agreeing was a miracle in itself. I had never been any happier in my entire life. I was going to play in the Lincolnton Optimist Tournament! Once again, my prayers were answered! I was not 100 percent, but I was able to play, and that was all that mattered to me.

In our first round game we were matched up against S. Ray Lowder, in a rematch of the previous season's championship tilt. My dad taped my fingers into a facsimile of a cast. I was so happy to be back on the basketball court with my teammates, he could have tied my hands behind my back. I was a little rusty throughout the game. I scored eighteen points, and we won 45–29, avenging the previous season's championship game loss. This effort catapulted me to within two points of the school scoring record. This was the same record that had seemed an impossible task several days earlier. It's amazing the way God works in our lives to teach us lessons and bring us back to earth.

The next evening we had our shot at the city champion, Battleground School, in the tournament semifinals. It was the city champions verses the county co-champions. This was the matchup the fans and players wanted! We won by an easy 46–22 score to gain a berth in the championship tilt the following evening. I finished the game with nineteen points, and in the process became not only the all-time leading scorer, but also the all-time leading rebounder in Central Junior High School's history.

The Lincolnton Optimist Championship game was held on Saturday evening. and we were once again facing the East Lincoln Optimist team made up of our rival Rock Springs players. Rock Springs had lost two players to age restrictions, but they had added Pat Jolley, a six-foot-six-inch sixth grader. The Lincolnton gym was packed for the title game. Both sides of the stands were full, and even the ends of the court were crowded, with standing room only. I was on the floor warming up and excited about being there, but I knew this would be a close game. I felt like we had the better team, though with Rock Spring's addition of the six-foot-six Jolly, everyone in attendance expected this matchup to be a barn burner. My right hand was sore from the previous night's game, but it didn't matter. I used my left hand to score thirteen points and pull down fourteen rebounds on the way to a 30–10 win. God's gift to me through the adversity of my injury was the ability to use my left hand the same as my right, something I could not do before the injury. A Lincolnton Optimist Tournament championship trophy finally belonged in the Central Junior High School trophy case. Later that evening, I was named to the All-Tournament team.

In the locker room, after the game, my dad gave every player a quart of soft drink to spew on one another. We had quite a "champagne" championship celebration that night.

Let the championship celebration begin! Another comeback is in the books.

After I showered and dressed, I walked back into the gym. It was nearly empty and the janitors were cleaning up. I thought back to that moment in the fifth grade when I felt sad and embarrassed for failing to make the Iron Station team. As I sat there, I thanked God for allowing me this comeback. At that moment I realized that the comeback was complete.

Two months later, at the Central Junior High School sports banquet I was named Basketball Most Valuable Player. Billy Packard, who would go on to become a famous college basketball announcer, presented my award. The morning after the sports banquet, I was walking in the school hallway when my English teacher, Mrs. Ervin, stopped me and said, "Quit being ashamed of being something special. You have worked hard to be who you are. Be proud and walk with your head up." From that moment on, I did just as she said, and it changed my entire outlook. I remember her as a great person, teacher, and friend. Thanks to that teacher's advice, I could now see where I was going, in more ways than one. My life's journey took me next to East Lincoln High School to see what kind of comebacks God had in store for me as a teen.

And don't say, "Now I can pay them back for what they've
done to me. I'll get even with them." Proverbs 24:29

One of the biggest lessons I learned during my years in high school
was the lesson of forgiveness. At that point in my young life, I had
never really been hurt in a way that made forgiving hard. During
my four years at East Lincoln, I found myself in a situation where
I honestly felt hate for the first time in my life. The story of this
injustice took many twists and turns before it made me a better
person and a stronger Christian.

It all started with my choice of high schools. A few weeks after
the Optimist Tournament, I received a visit from the basketball
coach of East Lincoln High School. I was called out of the lunchroom
by Mr. Shelton, brought to the gym, and put through basketball
drills, including the coach's famous machine-gun drill. I didn't
question any of this, I just enjoyed it. Where would I rather be: at
lunch or in the gym shooting hoops? This was not a hard choice
for me to make. Hey, I guess it was true. I'd rather play basketball
than eat.

Mr. Shelton and the varsity basketball coach at East Lincoln
High School were close friends. East Lincoln was a county school
that was twenty-three miles from my house. I lived in the Lincolnton
school district. Lincolnton was a city school that was three miles

from my house. My brother attended East Lincoln High School and played basketball there, so that was where I planned to attend. When Kevin started high school, we lived in the East Lincoln district, so he continued going to school there after we moved into our new home. The school board approved my decision to attend East Lincoln based on the fact that Kevin was already there. They recognized it would be a hardship on my parents for Kevin and me to be at different high schools.

I never realized the stir this decision would cause, as the Lincolnton high school faithful believed that I was coerced by the East Lincoln coaches to attend East Lincoln. This was not true. The LHS athletic director filed a complaint against me with the North Carolina High School Athletic Association, concerning the attendance guidelines. The NCHSAA upheld the school board's ruling. I believed that the issue was over with, but it was actually only the beginning.

My first two years of high school were filled with new and exciting learning experiences. I, like all fifteen-year-old boys, felt awkward, clumsy, had pimples, and loved the prettiest older girl in school, who barely knew my name. Or she may not have known it at all! I was happy to have basketball in my life as my outlet for all of these problems ... well, except for the pimples. Even basketball failed to do a thing for those pimples. The summer before my freshman year I attended Campbell College basketball school. Most of the East Lincoln players attended the school. On the bus trip to the college, a four-hour ride, I met my future best friend, Lewis "Re-C" Lowery. He was one of the top players on the Rock Springs squad. We roomed together at the camp, and from that point on we were best friends. Re-C and I remain close thirty three-years later.

During my freshman season I started on the tenth grade junior varsity team. We won the SD-7 Conference title with an 18–2 record. My sophomore season I also played on the junior varsity team, averaging nearly twenty-five points and fifteen rebounds per game. Re-C, Chuck Hartzog. and I moved up to the varsity team, as tenth graders, for the conference and district tournaments. By the end of my sophomore year, I was already looking forward to my junior year.

The summer between my sophomore and junior years proved to be long and stressful. It didn't start out that way. I once again went to basketball camp at Campbell College for a week. When I returned I played in pick-up games. If I couldn't find a game at Central Junior High, Lincolnton Recreation Center, or on some school playground, I played in my backyard. I counted the days until school started. None of this was stressful. The stress began in late June. That was when I found out that a good deed could cost me my entire basketball career.

On the evening of February 26, 1975, my sixteenth birthday, I received a phone call from a family friend who was the morning disc jockey for WLON radio, the local AM radio station. My mom had just finished preparing my birthday supper, the finale of which was a huge cake: my favorite homemade white cake piled high with mountains of rich, creamy homemade chocolate icing. Wayne asked me if I could play in a charity game that evening to help raise money for the North Carolina Children's Burn Center in Chapel Hill. The radio station had put together a local celebrity team to play against members of the Lincolnton fire department. All proceeds from the game went to the cost of building a new burn center for children. The game started less than an hour after I received the call, but my family agreed it was a good cause. We left our supper, figuring we could continue our celebration after we returned home. The game was played at the Lincolnton high school gym. In attendance were the high school's athletic director and its head basketball coach. The game was a charity event, so there was no admission charge, but donations were accepted at the door.

The WLON radio team consisted of disc jockeys, the mayor, city councilmen, television personalities, and me. I had a great time playing, as it was all in fun. I don't even remember who won. The game raised over three thousand dollars for the burn center. In June, four months after the charity game, I received a phone call from my high school basketball coach. Earlier in the day he had received a letter from the North Carolina High School Athletic Association (NCHSAA), stating that I had participated in a non-sanctioned game. The Lincolnton High School athletic director had filed the complaint against me with the NCHSAA for playing in the fundraiser. Because money was accepted at the door of the charity game, I broke NCHSAA rules. The letter went on to say that due to my participation, I was considered a professional and I would have to forfeit my final two seasons of high school eligibility. I was banned from playing my junior and senior years in high school!

I was devastated, as basketball was the ticket to all of my dreams. I felt as if in trying to help a children's hospital, I had lost everything I ever worked for or dreamed of. I had planned my entire life planned. Go to college and play basketball, play professional basketball, coach college basketball, and win a few titles. Forfeiting my last two seasons of high school basketball made this an almost impossible dream to achieve.

The local newspapers immediately picked up on the story. The WLON station manager offered to pay for an attorney. We were able to hire an attorney, who was also a North Carolina congressman from Gastonia, NC. In August 1975 my parents and I appeared in front of the NCHSAA Board of Appeals and presented our case. At the end of the appeal hearing, we adjourned, during which time I asked God to please allow the board to do what was just and rule in my favor. After two hours we were summoned back into the meeting room. The NCHSAA Board of Appeals announced that my suspension was reduced to the first six games of my junior year. Six games seemed like a harsh punishment for helping burned children, but I was too busy thanking God to worry about the six-game suspension.

During my junior year I thought the first six games would last for an eternity. I sat in the stands and watched our team start out with three wins and three losses. One of those losses came at the hands of the Lincolnton High School squad on a last-second half-court shot. My first game as a varsity starter came in the first game after Christmas break. It was an away game at Bunker Hill High School in Catawba. I was so excited to finally be playing again. The gym was full of fans from both schools, and I was a nervous wreck, but no more than before any other game. The first three-quarters of the game resembled anything except a successful comeback. I took one shot, missed it, and recorded three rebounds. I knew there were fans in the stands asking themselves, "What's the big deal about this Coffey kid coming back"? I was even asking myself the same question. At the start of the fourth quarter the tide began to turn in my favor. I scored sixteen of my team's nineteen fourth-quarter points, and added seven more rebounds. I really had come back. We won by twelve points. The next day the *Hickory Daily Record* headline read "Hot Coffey Burns Bears. " The comeback from my suspension was complete.

Still using that left hand to score another basket.

My junior year flew by. We finished the season third in the SD-7 conference, winning fifteen of nineteen games after Christmas. Along the way we upset Lincolnton on a last second shot by Chuck Hartzog, my old Central Junior High teammate. The season ended with a disappointing SD-7 tournament loss to those same rival Lincolnton Wolves. This was a low point for our team and for me individually, to be eliminated by the school that had caused my suspension. At that point my teammate and best friend Re-C and I sat down and mapped out our plan for getting to the coveted state tournament in our final season of high school basketball. This would be our last shot to come back and win a title. Our plan was to work harder, come back better, and reach our goal.

As I look back to those days, I note that we all had goals, all worked together as a team, and wanted the same things. Then, there really was no I in *team*. I think this is something that is now lacking, not only in the world of professional sports, but all the way down to the preteen level of competition. The ability to work as a team, like many other characteristics learned from sports, carries over into our adult lives. Today even preteens are taught and coached to do what is best for the player as an individual, and not what is best for the team. These same players, most of whom will never make it to the professional level of sports, have a hard time coping in the adult world, because they have been catered to and taught to look out only for themselves. Of the ones that do make it onto professional teams, many are not equipped to deal with the fame and fortune. The youth of today and tomorrow have to come back to the ways of past generations to learn the work ethic and teamwork that made this country what it was over one hundred years ago. The work ethic that we were taught by our parents and grandparents not only carried over into our extracurricular activities, but also throughout our adult lives. I remember this dedication for a goal most vividly when I think of my senior year in high school.

I began my senior year at East Lincoln hoping to win a SD-7 Conference basketball title, a District Seven basketball title, and hopefully a state championship. All of my friends and teammates shared the same goal. We went to basketball camp together, played together at any open gyms, and worked a lot on our own. It was total dedication toward a common goal. At the same time I was starting to focus on choosing a college. I received letters from over twenty universities, colleges, and junior colleges. While I enjoyed the attention, it was not individual goals I had in mind. I was only thinking of helping my teammates to reach our goal. The entire East Lincoln team worked together during the summer, and added Pat Jolley, now six feet ten inches tall, to a team with three returning starters. Everyone was excited, as the SD-7 conference had expanded to eleven teams.

The season started with three schools as the favorites: Bandy's High School, rival Lincolnton High School, and our East Lincoln Mustangs. The remaining eight teams were expected to battle for the five additional District Seven playoff spots. The newspapers and radio stations all predicted Bandy's to finish first in the conference for the third straight season. Lincolnton, the previous season's SD-7 runner-up, was loaded with former S. Ray Lowder and Battleground players. The Lincolnton Wolves also fielded several of my former teammates from Central Junior High School.

Through the first five games of the season, East Lincoln, Bandy's, and Lincolnton all had perfect records. The first "Big 3" matchup was held at East Lincoln, between East Lincoln and Lincolnton. The only time the game was close was at the outset. We took an early twenty-point lead and eventually won 65–54. The Lincolnton coach approached me, shook my hand, and told me I played well. To my disbelief, I held no ill feelings toward the Lincolnton coach. Maybe it was because I was so happy to beat them, or maybe God had led me to forgive this man and move on with my life, despite the way I had felt about him only months earlier.

Two weeks after defeating the Wolves, we had our first showdown with Bandy's High School. Both teams had begun the season with nine straight wins. State rankings, playoff seeds, and community pride were all at stake in the close-knit communities of Denver and Catawba. I arrived at the East Lincoln gym at five-thirty; the girls' game began at six-thirty. Over eight hundred people were standing outside the gymnasium. Every parking space was full, not only the gym parking area, but also the students' parking lot. Fans were even parking on the roadside in front of the school. When I walked through the front entrance, eight to ten excited fans pushed me aside and ran downstairs into the gym while the ticket taker yelled for them to stop. At the time, I thought they just wanted to get in the game without having to pay, but several seconds later, I understood they didn't want in for free, they just wanted in!

I peered down into the brightly lit gym from the glass windows above. The building was packed with parents, grandparents, students, and just fans in the community that would not miss such a game. Not only were the bleachers full, the stage doors were open, and the metal chairs for the overflow crowd were also all taken. The eight hundred fans waiting outside would not get a ticket to see the game. At the end of the third quarter of the girls' game, our players left the gym for our locker room. At the outside door of the gym, fans waved five-, ten-, and even twenty-dollar bills at us. The money was ours if we would just open the door for them to gain entrance. This was a small-town, big-time event. WLON 1050 radio was even broadcasting live.

Ultimately, this game would not be as close or as exciting as the fans anticipated. However, for the Mustangs it was highly exciting! East Lincoln defeated Bandy's 76–51, putting an end to any speculation as to who had the best team in the SD-7 conference. Never again would our team arrive at a game, home or away, that did not boast a gym full of orange- and green-clad East Lincoln fans, armed with cowbells, whistles, horns, and plenty of adrenaline to boost the Mustangs to nineteen school and individual records. After defeating Bandy's, the 1976–77

Mustangs won their next ten games, finishing the regular season with a perfect 20–0 record. Along the way to our twenty straight wins, we were able to put another loss on the records of rivals Lincolnton and Bandy's.

We continued our winning ways at the SD-7 Conference Tournament, and our team entered the District Seven Tournament with twenty-three straight wins. We needed three more wins to advance to the state tournament. During practice on the Monday after the conference tournament ended, I started feeling faint and my heart started racing. Within three minutes I was experiencing chest pains. The school nurse suggested I go to the hospital, due to the possibility of a murmur or other heart defect. My parents rushed me to the emergency room, where an EKG was done. The doctor arranged an appointment with the best heart specialist in the area.

The following day we went to the Sanger Clinic in Charlotte. I knew this had to be serious if we were going to the "big city" of Charlotte. I was given an EKG, stress test, and echocardiogram. During the test, I thought that regardless of the outcome, I had to play in the District 7 Tournament. I remembered my eighth grade hand injury and how God answered my prayers then. Once again I called on God and asked Him to please help me through what I feared was another life-ending crisis. Still I wondered what I had done to deserve this punishment. Even as a teen I was aware that God punishes us for our sins, just as parents punish their children so that they will be safe and grow to be responsible adults. I wondered which sin this bump in the road was for.

Until this setback, this had been the best year of my life. I had a great relationship with my parents. My parents and grandparents attended every game, along with Mrs. Connie Cornwell, a dear family friend of my father's parents. My nine-year-old sister, Sue Ellen, wore an East Lincoln cheerleader's outfit made by our mom, with matching saddle shoes, just like the Mustang cheerleaders wore. She cheered at every game. Each game was a Coffey family affair.

The doctor finally came in with my test results. He explained that the pain was not coming from my heart itself. I was having spasms in the muscles surrounding my heart. This was not a fatal defect, just something I needed to be aware of. He stated that there was no reason I shouldn't continue to play basketball. I jumped for joy, hugged the doctor, hugged my mom, and then asked my mom drive me straight to practice. It was great news, and I thanked God once again for His mercy in allowing me the opportunity to continue playing basketball.

Before the first round of the District 7 tournament began, the SD-7 All Conference team was announced. My friend Re-C and I were named to the SD-7 All-Conference team. It was later announced that I was named First Team All Gazette-land and High School all-American. I was joined on these lists by future NBA all-stars James Worthy, Eric "Sleepy" Floyd, and Mark Aquire. My family was very proud, as I was the first Lincoln County player to ever receive either of the latter two honors.

Thursday night of the tournament finally arrived, and I was on the court, muscle spasms and all. The first round of the tournament was much like the regular season; we defeated West Lincoln 78–46. This set up a District 7 semifinal showdown against Lincolnton. Having lost to us three times already, the Lincolnton coaching staff devised a new game plan to derail the Mustang express. The plan was to hold the basketball and make the game as short as possible. It was a good plan in theory, but it still remains the most boring game I ever participated in. Thanks to point guard Alan Brotherton and good ole Re-C, we held a 16–10 advantage at the end of the first half, despite the stalling tactics. We started the second half with an 8–0 run to open a fourteen-point lead. That put an end to Lincolnton's unsuccessful game plan. The semifinal victory cemented a four game sweep of the Wolves that season. The District 7 championship match was set. A fourth win against Bandy's High School was all that stood between our team and our dream.

The game was played on my birthday, February 26, exactly three years after I played in the benefit game that led to so much grief. Fans packed the gym at Lenior Rhyne College in Hickory, NC. The old two-story structure was filled to capacity. This time, there was room for those eight hundred fans that had been turned away at East Lincoln months earlier. Bandy's sported a 21–4 record. Three of Bandy's losses were compliments of the Mustangs, with each game being closer than the previous. Still, we all knew the past was insignificant and had no bearing on our reaching our goal now.

In the championship tilt, we started slowly. I picked up two quick fouls trying to guard James McCleave, one of the leading scorers, and best players in the state. At the end of the first quarter, we trailed 16–10. We came back in the second quarter, but were still behind by three at the halfway point. During halftime, there was no bickering or finger pointing among my teammates. We were a team and we would stick together, win or lose. At the end of the third quarter we took our first lead, 52–50, on a Pat Jolley monster slam dunk. Alan Brotherton made a steal and I hit a jump shot to put us up by four points.

This shot put us up by 4 points. We would not trail again.

We never trailed again and went on to win by thirteen points, 79–66. We had won ourselves a trip to Durham, NC, for the state tournament.Everyone of my team mates and all of the students, parents, and East Lincoln fans in attendance were exhausted from the excitement of the game and the 26 game winning streak. Despite the exhaustion we were excited about the victory and ready to celebrate.

Left to right Alan Brotherton, Coaches John Stiver and Ted Bright, Pat Jolley, Lewis "Re-C" Lowery, me, and Robby Link. Back row Tim Lawing. My birthday and we beat Bandys to go to the state tournament

After the game our team stopped at McDonald's for my birthday party and a victory celebration. My parents surprised us with a birthday cake, and everyone at McDonald's, employees and patrons alike, enjoyed cake and celebrated the victory along with us. The next week was a week of practice and preparation for the state title. The game was played in Durham, about three hours away. The school chartered two buses for the fans, and both were filled to capacity the first day reservations went on sale. The morning of the game, the entire student body, friends, and families gave our team a pep rally and sent us on our way to

Durham. On the long trip there, my favorite English teacher and I played nickel and dime poker. I lost two dollars to her. I knew my parents would not approve, not because I lost the money, but because we were not allowed to gamble. In my opinion, it was just a good way to pass the time on the long trip. I figured there was no harm, and my parents would never find out anyway.

We arrived at the Durham YMCA at three thirty in the afternoon for a shootaround. After checking into our hotel, we ate a pre-game meal at five o'clock—steak, baked potato, salad, and dessert. We were treated like kings. This ritual felt odd to me, since I always ate at three thirty on game days. My mom and dad always had a steak, hamburgers, hot dogs, or some other big meal for me. That night I learned why a pre-game meal at three thirty was better than one two hours before game time. By the start of the game, my teammates and I were more ready for a nap than for playing for the state championship.

We faced a very athletic Wake Forest-Rolesville team and committed sixteen turnovers in a sluggish, for us, first half. At the end of the first half, we trailed by seventeen points. We came out "hungry" in the second half and outscored Wake Forest 22–3 in the third quarter. The game went back and forth in the final quarter, and we were defeated 68–65. My mom came up to me after the game and wasn't feeling sorry for me as I expected. She let me know that God was punishing me for gambling on the bus ride to Durham. My first thought was, "How did she find out?" God must have told her, I decided, but later I found out it was not God, just a nosy cheerleader. At the time though, I thought that maybe she was right. We had had the better team and had somehow found a way to lose. Maybe this was my punishment for gambling.

The next week the bitterness of the loss had not diminished;

five years later the pain was still there; and thirty-three years later, it still makes me sad to remember that rainy evening in Durham.

While that seemed to be the lowest point of my life, the following week's news would only make my life worse. I failed my French class for the second time, which translated into no big-time college basketball in my near future. My choices were reduced to either a NCAA Division II college or a NJCAA junior college. I opted for junior college as a means to advance to a NCAA Division I college.

My junior high and high school years were great learning experiences, with setbacks and comebacks along the way. I felt I was leaving high school on a low note, losing the state championship and a chance to play Division I college basketball in a short two-week span. I did not realize that the required comebacks and the successes that followed would be a source of strength, leading to more important comebacks many years later.

I entered Caldwell Community College in the fall of 1977 and learned that being on my own was not as easy as I had imagined. I had a work-study job grading papers for the auto mechanics instructor. I also took fourteen credit hours, but mostly I played basketball and partied. My one season at Caldwell was an eye-opening experience, as the team started out with only one win in seven games. During my junior high and high school careers, a total of six years, I competed on teams that compiled an overall record of 104 wins and 20 losses. By the end of my first college season, we had lost twenty games while winning only six. Losing was something I was not accustomed to. I averaged twenty points and twelve rebounds a game, and I decided I was not ever going back to Caldwell Community College. I wanted to try my hand at the NBA and the professional basketball career that I always dreamed of.

I have told you these things , so that in me you may have peace. In this world you will have trouble. But take heart! I have overcome the world. John 16:33

During the next three years, I got married and my first child, Brooke, was born. At the moment of her birth I knew what it was like to love your own child, and to be responsible for another human's life. This was something I had never experienced, and there is no way anybody can explain this love to someone else. Following Brooke's birth, I worked full-time and played in several open basketball leagues simultaneously. I always believed that if I kept practicing and playing and continued to improve. I would eventually realize my dream of fun, fame, and fortune in the NBA.

I began training harder than ever, and a friend of mine suggested that I consider weight training. I had never thought of weight lifting for basketball. It was always discouraged during my teen years, as it would "hurt your shooting touch." I joined a local gym frequented by national level bodybuilders and professional athletes, and started lifting weights six days a week. I ran seven miles every morning and sprinted two miles every evening. In January 1981, an international scout from Carlsbad, California, representing Basketball Players International, contacted me. He had watched me play in an open league national tournament in Columbia, SC.

He invited me to attend a professional tryout scouted by twenty international team scouts and eight NBA teams. My chance had finally arrived. I was going to Washington, DC, to try out in front of NBA coaches and scouts.

In the first six months of my weight training, I gained fifteen pounds of muscle, and the extra mass transformed my basketball abilities. I was faster, stronger, and jumped higher than I ever had before. While I was preparing for my upcoming tryout, a bodybuilder at the gym approached me. He explained to me that if I wanted to get stronger at a faster rate, I should use anabolic steroids. I knew about steroids, but they were a hushed topic at the time. Whenever I thought of steroids, I thought of football players. Little did I know that many years later, baseball players, track stars, wrestlers, and, yes, basketball players would be using steroids illegally. I asked him questions about the results and the cost. For one hundred fifty dollars I was able to purchase a six-week cycle of oral tablets and injectable steroids.

The next day I paid the bodybuilder and picked up my first cycle of steroids, which included three different oral tablets—Winstrol, Dyanabol, and Anavar—and one vial of testosterone and ten syringes. The recommended dosage for each drug was two and one half milligrams per day. The bodybuilder told me to take ten milligrams, four times the recommended amount. I added to that one cc of the testosterone per week. Within three weeks I had packed on another ten pounds of muscle and saw gains in strength with every workout. My bench press went from a maximum lift of 200 pounds to 280 pounds within weeks.

I was in love with the new drugs and started taking higher dosages. After all, if ten milligrams per day produced such great results, what would fifteen milligrams per day accomplish? Along with the added strength and endurance came a person I never knew existed. That person was me, but was not Jeff Coffey. I quit caring about going to church, about God, about my job, or my family. I was obsessed with getting stronger and preparing for my lifelong dream, a shot at the National Basketball Association.

In August of 1981 I was nine months away from my big week, a trip to Washington, DC, to try out for the NBA. I was playing the best basketball of my life. I took a week off to prepare for my tryout, traveling to Myrtle Beach, SC, for intense workouts and relaxation. On August 20 I went to the gym, worked out for two hours, and ran two miles on the beach, all before nine AM. By nine thirty I was experiencing excruciating pain in the center of my back. Within five minutes, my left arm was aching, and I was sweating profusely. I went to a local convenience store and bought a bottle of aspirin. An hour later the pain became so intense, I went to Grand Strand Medical Center.

Within two minutes of entering the emergency room, I was on a stretcher with an IV in one arm, blood was being drawn from the other arm, and I had been placed on oxygen. Before eleven o'clock, the doctor brought me the devastating news: I had suffered a heart attack and was being admitted to the Intensive Care Unit. He seemed surprised that a twenty-three-year-old in great health could have a heart attack, but I knew that the steroids had caused the attack. Still, I hoped I would be out of the hospital by the next day to continue my training. The doctor explained that I had suffered permanent heart damage. In six weeks, the cardiologist said, I could start walking a quarter of a mile a day. There would be no professional basketball tryouts now or ever. He told me very bluntly that I was lucky to be alive.

I was months away from the biggest opportunity of my life,

and I could not even walk a quarter of a mile. I was totally and completely devastated. I was placed in intensive care, and the next morning I suffered a second heart attack. I was a patient at Grand Strand Hospital in Myrtle Beach for one week, and then my parents drove me to Grace Hospital in Columbia, SC, for a heart catheterization.

The evening before the procedure, I was visited by a nun. She was the first nun I had ever seen, except for the flying one on television, and this nun looked nothing like that one. My nun was not tall, slim, beautiful, and wearing white. My nun was four feet tall and round, but she was still a beautiful sight to me. I sensed that she was a holy person, and I was happy that she prayed for me. When she finished praying, a sense of peace came over me. I quit worrying altogether and was very relaxed, until a few minutes later when a nurse came in and said, "I'm here to shave you." Huh?

The next morning I was wheeled to the operating room, where the heart catheterization was performed. The afternoon after the surgery my doctor delivered the good news. There was no permanent damage. The doctor said that I could begin walking short distances in two weeks and work my way up from there. Within three weeks of being discharged, I was running seven miles a day and weight training four days a week—minus the steroids! Nine months after the hospitalization, in June 1982, I attended the professional tryouts in Silver Springs, Maryland.

My recovery was certainly a miracle, a gift sent from God. While I realize there are many people who don't believe in them, a miracle is the only term I can use to explain my comeback. I suffered two heart attacks, and nine months later competed for a position in professional basketball. I believe God used this setback to slow me down and force me to take a look at my life. It worked!

I started back to church, became close to my family again, and returned to living a Christian life. While a Christian life by no definition means sinless, it does mean doing our best to love one another and to treat one another as Christ treats us, with love and forgiveness.

I was selected at the tryouts for the NBA summer league team. I played for Coach Gene Shue of the then Washington Bullets, now known as the Wizards. I averaged sixteen points, six rebounds, and six assists per game. From that exposure I was offered several professional opportunities. That comeback is one I was very thankful for and very proud of. I never made it to the NBA, but I did get within one step. I felt I had fulfilled a dream, and I was satisfied with a successful playing career. It was time for me to hang up my sneakers, or so I thought.

Ten years later, I tried out for the Continental Basketball Association's Rockford Lightning at thirty-two years of age. As a result of that tryout, I was offered a contract to play in the World Basketball League. I turned the opportunity down, as I was married with two daughters and three sons to support. Once again I felt I had accomplished all I could as a player, and my competitive playing days were now a memory. From the fourth grade tournament at Asbury Elementary School; to the records I broke at Central Junior High School; to the Lincolnton Optimist Tournament title; to East Lincoln High School, Caldwell Community College, and my post-college days, my basketball career is something that I will always have fond memories of. I learned from the experiences and gained strength from the comebacks. The only basketball dream that remained was to coach at the college level.

Coaching at that level seemed impossible. My wife Anna Marie and I sold our share of a health club, with the intention of opening a restaurant or buying a restaurant franchise. The opportunity to coach college basketball never entered my mind again. I had a business plan, but God had a different plan for me and my life, which included learning that only His justice is real and just.

Free me from the trap that is set for me, for you are my refuge. Psalm 31:4

While justice is real and at times still exists, I learned the hard way that the justice in our country in most cases has become an afterthought with a lack of common sense. There are killers, rapists, child molesters, and worse walking our streets today and still committing crimes, because their rights were violated during their arrest or their judicial proceedings. The court's decision to set them free had nothing to do with guilt or innocence. Whatever happened to the belief that if a person commits a crime, he is punished for it? What about the victim's rights? It should not matter what is said or not said, guilty is guilty! Does it change a person's guilt if that person is given the Miranda warning and told they have the right to remain silent? How can we as a nation justify turning these criminals back into society to commit the same acts all over again? In the 1800s and before, if a person killed another person, he was tried in such a manner that truth was the only thing that mattered. If a criminal was tried and convicted, the sentence was carried out swiftly. Today, a person charged with first degree murder may stand trial a year or more after the offense; and if convicted, might wait another four to ten years before he is punished. That is the reason our crime rates are the highest in history and rising.

On the other end of the spectrum, not all law-enforcement personnel and judges really care about true justice, but only about a conviction. For decades policemen, detectives, attorneys, and judges have been taking bribes that determined the outcome of cases. Since the discovery of DNA, many wrongly convicted people have been released from prison, with no doubt more to come in the future. These are cases where there was little investigation and, due to a false assumption, another person's life was destroyed. I had my own personal experience that led me to my beliefs about today's justice system.

I have always wanted to own a restaurant. I love restaurant management, though I can't explain why the business interests me so much. I like taking orders, cooking, being under pressure to get food out in a timely manner, and getting the order correct. I love predicting sales volumes, training employees, and, most of all, customer service.

I started working in the food service industry in 1988 for Domino's Pizza. My intention was to learn the trade and buy my own franchise. The company rule was that you had to manage a store before you could buy one. My career began as an assistant manager, and within several months, I became a store manager. I loved the business. I was soon transferred and put in charge of a store in Hickory, NC. When I arrived at this location, I found that it was one of the poorest revenue-producing stores in the industry. There were many weeknights when we opened at 4:00 PM and closed at 11:00 PM and received fewer than ten orders. I worked as a manager at this location for over a year and learned lessons about business and marketing comebacks.

One year after I had arrived at the Hickory location, its business had doubled. The revenue grew due to my marketing plan, which included special promotions , a quality product , and improved customer service. My entire family helped me reach my sales goal by hanging coupons on the doors of every house and apartment within ten miles of the store. With all the strategies in place, the store grew at a record pace. As a reward for my success, I was transferred to a larger struggling store in nearby Conover. Several months later that franchise was sold. I was given the option of transferring out of state to Clemson, SC, to work for a different franchise owner, or lose my job altogether.

I left the store for five days to look at the new location in Clemson, and to make a decision concerning my career path with Domino's. I was not happy with the situation in Clemson and decided not to accept the transfer. My family and I were disappointed and scared at the thoughts of our options. The night before we left Clemson, I asked God to help me make the best decision and to lead me in the right direction. The following morning, on our way home, I stopped at Pizza Hut Inc. in Charlotte. I was interviewed and hired to open and manage a brand new store, a delivery unit in Statesville, NC.

When I returned home, I telephoned my regional manager and informed him that I was giving the company one week's notice. The following day he was already present at the store when I arrived. He informed me that I was being transferred back to the original Hickory store for my final week at Domino's. Several hours later he came to the Hickory store and informed me that I did not need to work a one-week notice; he already had a manager for the store. At the time I felt all of this was odd, but I was happy to be starting my new job with Pizza Hut.

I thanked God for allowing me to make another of life's required comebacks. I had gone from a situation in which I would have had to move and leave my family, or lose my job. God had guided me to a job with a higher salary and better benefits. Around this same time, God blessed us with our youngest son, Kyle. We were all very happy, until three weeks later when I received a phone call from my former employer.

The former franchise owner of Domino's Pizza stated that they were missing six deposits, four from Conover and two from Hickory, all totaling nearly nine thousand dollars. The owner claimed I was responsible for the missing deposits, and he was giving me thirty days to repay the money. I knew I had not taken the deposits and had no idea what had happened to them. For the next thirty days the Domino's management staff harassed my family and me. They called my wife and children and told them that I needed to repay the nine thousand dollars that I stole or I would be going to jail for a long time.

Two months later, in December 1990, I was sitting in my living room with my wife and children watching Monday Night Football, when we heard a knock at the door. My wife answered the door to find two city detectives, weapons drawn, standing there. There were also two uniformed police officers at the back door. All this manpower to arrest me for the embezzlement of nine thousand dollars. I was searched, handcuffed, and driven to the police station. Two detectives, one from each town where the thefts occurred, questioned me for over four hours. I was told the dates of the missing deposits, and I knew that the four from the Conover store were from the days I was in Clemson, SC. The two missing deposits from the Hickory store baffled me, as I normally made the deposits and I knew they all had been handled properly. After explaining to the detectives that I had been out of town during the time of the Conover store thefts, I was informed that the deposits had been held in the store safe until I came back from Clemson. I said I was unaware of this. Moreover, I had been transferred on the day of my return and had never entered the Conover store safe. I was then questioned about the two missing deposits from the Hickory store. One of the deposits was from my final evening there, when my regional manager relieved me of my duties and took over the store.

Although I explained all of this, the detectives still thought I was responsible for the thefts. A case of "We think you did it, so we won't investigate or look any further." I offered to take a polygraph test, but I was not allowed the opportunity. After the interviews concluded, I was released on bail. I returned home that night to scared children and a very worried wife. At that point I could not imagine how or why this had happened to me. Why would God do this to me? I went to church; I always tried to teach my children about Christian practices; I volunteered in the community; and most importantly, I did not steal the deposits. I did not understand that this was not being God's will, but the actions of other human beings that were causing my family this pain. At this point in my life, I grew closer to God than I had ever been before. I was still working for Pizza Hut and enjoyed my job, but the eighteen months that followed would require another comeback. This was a comeback that if unsuccessful could result in two felony convictions, twenty years in prison, and a twenty-thousand-dollar fine.

The day after I was arrested, I contacted and met with a local attorney. He indicated that the evidence in the case was neither in my favor nor against me. He said it would be up to a jury to sort through it all and make a decision. The attorney requested a six-thousand-dollar retainer fee. Since I did not have an extra six thousand dollars lying around, I decided I would depend on God to once again guide me through yet another ordeal.

The trial was delayed for over a year. In August 1991, a trial date was finally set. My first appearance was in September 1991. At the initial hearing, I pled not guilty and was assigned a public defender by the name of Mr. Dettores. I met with Mr. Dettores the following afternoon and went through the entire case with him. He requested and obtained the evidence from the district attorney's office. Over the next week we worked together on my defense. My trial date was set for October 14, 1991, at the Catawba County Courthouse.

On October 10 I received a call from Mr. Dettores. The district attorney was offering me a plea bargain. I would plead guilty to the charges, and the charges would be reduced to a misdemeanor theft charge. In exchange for the plea, I would receive a five-year suspended sentence and pay Domino's nine thousand dollars over a five-year period. I immediately turned down the plea bargain offer and prepared for court. I was scared, but I put my trust in God and tried not to think about what could possibly lie ahead.

The morning of October 14 finally arrived, and by seven thirty in the morning our house was full of family, friends, and my parents. We drove to the courthouse, and I prayed most of the way there. That I could be convicted of something I did not do and leave my wife and five children for a prison term, were thoughts I tried to suppress.

The courtroom resembled the Perry Mason courtrooms I remembered from television. I met with my attorney and then anxiously waited for the clock to reach nine thirty so my trial could begin. While I was sitting in the lobby, the Domino's regional manager and three more of Domino's upper management team entered the courtroom carrying boxes overflowing with documents. They all walked in with smiles on their faces, full of confidence.

The first day was spent selecting the jury and opening arguments. On the second day, testimony began. The prosecution called the three Domino's upper management employees to the witness stand, as well as my former regional manager. He testified that he had informed me of the deposits in the Conover safe when I arrived from Clemson, which I knew was not true. He further testified that he left the Conover store before I did on the day I was transferred to the Hickory location, which was my last day of employment. This was also untrue.

In the meantime my attorney contacted a former Domino's employee who had been working in Conover the afternoon I was transferred. Karen was a student at the University of North Carolina in Chapel Hill. She informed Mr. Dettores that she had seen the regional manager remove the deposits from the safe after I had left the Conover store. She saw him place the deposits in a plastic garbage bag. My attorney informed the judge that he had discovered an eyewitness to the crime, and he requested a one-day delay in the trial so that Karen could testify. Karen was taking final exams and could not miss them to attend the judicial proceedings. The judge ruled against me; there would be no delay.

At that point, I lost respect for our justice system. I was on trial for a crime I did not commit, I had proof of who had committed the crime, but a delay was not granted so the truth could be presented. I was troubled and confused. The judge and the jury had the opportunity to hear who had really stolen the deposits, yet the judge did not think it was important enough to delay the trial for one day. I was starting to see that justice was not always what it seemed, and that the good guys were not always the good guys.

Mr. Dettores told me not to worry, that he could delay the trial in his own way, which he did. On several occasions throughout the day, Mr. Dettores asked for extra time to review the many Domino's documents being presented.

As day two drew to a close, the Domino's regional manager was on the witness stand. During his testimony he bragged about Domino's security systems, and stated there was no possible way that anyone could come into the store and take the deposits. He further testified that nobody had access to the store keys or the safe keys, except the manager and the assistant manager.

The second day ended with his testimony, and as soon as court was adjourned my parents left for Chapel Hill to pick up my star witness, Karen. I was feeling a little better. Despite the lack of concern for true justice, the judge was unable to prevent her testimony. Throughout the trial I prayed more than I ever prayed before. Getting cut from the Iron Station tryouts, the broken fingers in the eighth grade, the Optimist Tournament, and my high school career seemed so small and unimportant now. However, those small events early in my life had prepared me and given me the strength, determination, and faith to come back from this potentially life-changing curve ball.

The following morning Karen arrived at the courthouse, and it was as if God had sent an angel to rescue me. Day three of the trial began with Karen taking the witness stand. Mr. Dettores opened by recapping the previous day's testimony by the regional manager, particularly the security system and the key system. Mr. Dettores then asked Karen several questions concerning her employment at Domino's. He asked if she had ever been a manager or an assistant manager, to which she replied, "No, sir." He asked if she had ever had a set of keys to the store. She replied, "Yes, sir, and as a matter of fact, I still have them!" She pulled her keys out of her pocket and held them up for the judge, jury, and courtroom spectators to see. On her key ring were keys to the store and the safe. She further testified that on the day the deposits disappeared, she saw the regional manager remove the deposits from the safe after I had left for the Hickory store. He then placed the deposits in a plastic trash liner and took them out of the store with the trash.

Everyone in the entire courtroom was dumbfounded and shocked. It was just like an episode of *Perry Mason* or *Matlock*. I thought the judge would make the regional manager take the witness stand, so he could be questioned and would confess, and this nightmare would all be over with. Real life, though, is not as simple as the television shows.

The prosecution did not ask Karen any questions, but did request a short delay to regroup. The judge granted this delay. The district attorney sent Mr. Dettores, a new plea bargain offer. They were willing to drop all of the charges, but I would still be required to repay the stolen money. I considered the plea bargain, because by declining the offer I was putting my life and my family's future back in the jury's hands. I prayed about this offer, but did not consult with anyone except the good Lord before declining the deal. While I no longer trusted law enforcement or judges, I still had faith that God would see to it that justice prevailed.

I testified on my own behalf and was cross-examined for an hour and twenty minutes. At the end of my testimony, both sides gave their closing arguments. The jury was instructed about the laws as they pertained to this case. Court was adjourned at 4:10 in the afternoon. Anna Marie, my parents, and I sat around and did a lot of praying. If I was found guilty, I would receive my sentence that afternoon and be sent straight to jail. At 4:45 PM, court was called back into session. A verdict had been reached.

Everyone entered the courtroom, and we were asked to stand while the judge entered. The jury followed. I looked at the seven men and five women who had determined my fate and my family's future. From their faces, I could not tell the verdict. Some jurors looked at me as they entered the courtroom, while others would not make eye contact .The judge asked the jury foreman to read the verdict, and I was asked to stand.

The foreman stood and read the judgment."We, the jury, find the defendant Jeffery Lyle Coffey ... not guilty of count one, embezzlement from the Conover, North Carolina, location. Not guilty of count two, embezzlement from the Hickory, North Carolina, location."

I immediately thanked God and hugged my attorney, my wife, and my parents. The judge thanked the jury and asked them to meet with him after court adjourned. I was told that I was free to go. After court adjourned, my wife, parents, and I waited in the parking lot to thank the jury. The foreman told us that the judge, following the trial, had told the jury that this was the worst prepared case and worst case of false arrest he had ever witnessed. Apparently the detectives had taken the Domino's management team at their word and never questioned any witnesses, including Karen.

This was one comeback I was glad to have behind me. This event served to further strengthen my faith and bring me closer to God, for which I was thankful. It also taught me that everyone is human and makes mistakes. The detectives made mistakes, the district attorney made mistakes, and the judge made mistakes. While these people did not truly pursue justice, the jury did, and God led them to a just decision. While I lost faith in our judicial system during the trial, the jury and Mr. Dettores showed me that the judicial system actually worked, and despite some bad decisions, justice had prevailed!

VII

The king will reply, "I tell you the truth, whatever you did for one of the least of these brothers of mine, you did for me." Matthew 25:40

As I view our society, watch the news, and read the newspapers, my conclusion is we need to return to an older way of life, to a nation that consisted of a neighbor helping another neighbor. It may not be sharing land to grow crops, or helping a neighbor build a log cabin, like the really old days. Instead it could be giving a neighbor a job, or helping with bills when someone is unemployed. A true coming back to charity is essential for our nation to return to what it once was. By coming back, I mean coming back to an older way of existence, a complete overhaul. Instead of giving money to organizations, we need to start helping those closer to us, as close as next door or down the street. It is a personal way to insure that our resources are spent the way we intend and that that go to those who truly need them. No middleman to take his share before any of the needy receive theirs.

In the past we gave our contributions to major organizations in hopes that the money was well spent. Recently, these same organizations have come under fire for abusing the funds with which they were entrusted. The United Way has suffered major scandals in New York City, Charlotte, NC, and Washington, DC, that involve criminal activity and questionable ethics. These are not the only charitable organizations making promises that they do not fulfill. There are thousands of these organizations nationwide. They are promising everything from helping widows of policemen to feeding starving children. "For thirty-five cents a day, you can feed a starving child." That's after the celebrity spokesperson is compensated, the television ad is paid for, the operator ready to take your call and all employees are paid. After all of these expenses are deducted, how much of the thirty-five cents a day is left to feed the children? If you want to feed a starving child, buy a bag of groceries and take it to a needy family. That way every dime will go toward feeding those starving children.

In my own life I have experienced the power of God's charity and how much can be done on a local level to help others. In 1992 I was managing a fast-food restaurant. One summer afternoon, I was helping unload supplies when a truck driver dropped a forty-pound case on top of me and injured my left shoulder. I went to the emergency room for X-rays, thinking it was broken. The emergency room doctor scheduled an MRI. The following morning I had the MRI, and was told that I had a severely torn rotator cuff. They put my arm in a sling and told me the injury might require surgery.

This was a tough time for my family and me, as workers compensation does not pay all the bills. We were never wealthy—with five children it's hard to be wealthy—but we were always blessed with a comfortable life. All of a sudden, we knew what it was like to be poor. Hoping to avoid surgery, I had physical therapy for four months, but in October my doctor determined that surgery was needed. By December I had been on workers compensation for seven months. My wife had always stayed home with our children, as we both felt this was much more important than financial wealth. She found a job at a nearby plant nursery, so we were able to continue to make ends meet. With Christmas fast approaching, Anna and I wondered how we would explain to the kids that this would not be the typical Coffey Christmas. Not only was I unable to work, but one car needed new tires and the other car's transmission had recently dropped out. The washing machine was broken, and we had just enough money to pay the bills. There would not be a stack of presents under the tree this year, and very little in the way of a holiday meal. Anna's parents and my parents, along with aunts and uncles, always sent gifts, but Santa was going to be a little short this year.

Several Sundays before Christmas, our son Jeremy took an angel from the angel tree at our church. The angel tree had the names of underprivileged children and what they were asking Santa to bring them. In the past we had always supplied the needs of four or five angels on the tree. This year we might be able to provide for one. Jeremy had been telling us for months that all he wanted for Christmas was a bicycle. It just so happened that the child he selected from the angel tree also wanted a bicycle. We explained to Jeremy that we could not help the child on the angel tree. We told him to take the angel back to church and find a gift we could afford. We would do our best to get him his bike for Christmas, but there was no possible way we could afford two bicycles. At the time, we didn't even know how we would afford one for Jeremy.

*Jeremy asking Santa Claus to bring him a new bicycle
and then Jeremy gave it to a needy child*

Jeremy told us to tell Santa Claus to take his bicycle and give it to the needy child. Because of that, Anna began working extra hours at the greenhouse, and we bought the bike for the angel tree. When we took it to the church, Anna told a friend about Jeremy's decision to donate his bicycle. The following week all of us went with the youth group to sing Christmas carols at the homes of the families that were having gifts delivered. When we arrived at the house of the young boy who had requested the bicycle, Jeremy was able to see the look on his face when his wish came true. Jeremy never said anything else about his bicycle.

The following week, on the Monday before Christmas, a church member arrived at our front door. He owned a Firestone store, and he had come to tell us that he wanted to donate all of the parts and labor to fix our cars, including four new tires. An hour or so later, the Sears repairman arrived at our house and told us that a church member had asked him to come by and repair our washing machine. Two days before Christmas, another church member came to our house with a country ham, a spiral ham, and all the fixings for a fabulous Christmas dinner. That same evening, two more church members arrived and asked Anna and me to come outside. When we went out, we saw presents for the kids, including a new bicycle for our Jeremy. What had once seemed like the worst Christmas ever became one of the best, and certainly the most memorable, in my life.

Thanks to the charity and caring of local people on a local level, we were able to come back, and we are now the ones able to help others in need. The type of charity that Jeremy and the members of St. Joseph Catholic Church in Newton, NC, showed that Christmas is the type we all need to practice on a daily basis. We should not have to pay a person millions of dollars in compensation to decide where our money will go. Let's come back to the past and help one another. After all, one of the two major commandments taught by Jesus is "love thy neighbor."

VIII

I know the plans I have for you, declares the Lord,
plans to prosper and not to harm you, plans to give
you hope and a future. Jeremiah 29:11

Everyone in every walk of life has dreams, goals, and self-expectations. These change as we grow older and mature, and as our situations change. Sometimes we work hard to achieve a goal, only to lose it later. We can't ask God why He did this to us, or why He let that happen to us. The accomplishments that we work hard for can be taken from us by other people who are just like us. Again, all human beings have the freedom to make choices and decisions, and often those decisions will affect the lives of others, including you and me. During my lifetime this happened to me twice in succession. I reached my life's goal of becoming a college basketball coach, only to lose both opportunities due to the actions of others.

During my shoulder rehabilitation period, my physician indicated that I needed to find another occupation, where no heavy lifting was required. I decided to enroll at Catawba Valley Community College in Hickory, because I wanted to become a sportswriter and needed to brush up on my writing skills. While taking classes in the fall semester, I read an article in the *Hickory Daily Record* that CVCC was going to resurrect its basketball program after an eight-year hiatus. I contacted the CVCC student services director, Bo Glenn, to interview for the coaching position. I was given the job of head coach, finally realizing my dream of being a college basketball coach. It's still amazing to me that God put me in the right place at the right time.

I was determined to take advantage of the situation God had allowed me and make my goal of being a NCAA Division I head coach a reality. My first task was to put together a schedule and hold tryouts for the CVCC team. CVCC was a member of the Western Tar Heel Conference, which was made up of six junior colleges, including Caldwell Community College, where I played in 1977. CVCC had no gymnasium, so we met at the local recreation center for practice. I scheduled games anywhere we could find a facility available. I planned practices around the pickup games in the afternoons at the recreation center.

We started the season with eight players. Our first game was an away game against Wilkes Community College. It was a tight game, and we eventually lost by three points. I was disappointed at the outcome, but in the same sense, excited to have coached my first college basketball game. I went home that night and wrote my own newspaper story. I faxed it in to the local newspapers, and the next day it was printed. CVCC basketball was on the map, barely!

The following week, while the team was practicing at the recreation center, I met a young man by the name of Dale Wicker. Dale was six feet seven inches tall and very thin. He played against our team in a scrimmage and played well. He informed me that he was registering at CVCC for the winter term, so I invited him to join the team. Little did I know that this would help pave the way not only for a successful season of basketball for CVCC , but also for Dale's own comeback. While speaking with Dale and his father, I learned that Dale had been cut from his high school team every year. He worked hard, but the coach felt that Dale did not have the necessary skills to contribute to the team. Being cut from the high school team every year disappointed Dale and his family, to say the least.

The first day Dale attended practice, we were going through defensive drills. My three-year-old son Kyle attended practice with me every day. On that afternoon, Kyle told me that he had to go to the restroom, so he used the one located in the gym. Several minutes later the whole team, during a drill, started laughing. I turned around to see Kyle, pants down around his ankles, yelling, "Daddy, I'm done." One of the players knew how much I tried to emulate former UNC and Hall of Fame coach, Dean Smith; and he blurted out, "What would Dean do now, Coach?" This was just one of many comical moments of our first-year program and this first-year coach.

After Dale Wicker joined the CVCC squad, we won ten straight games. In late January, we faced Caldwell Community College at the Newton Recreation Center. It was a Saturday evening game. The local youth basketball teams were admitted free of charge. In addition, the local youth cheerleaders were invited to cheer for CVCC. It was going to be the biggest game of the year. The morning of the game my wife and I decided we needed to dye our white uniform bottoms red to match our red jerseys. The team had new red uniform tops, but the shorts had not arrived. After the first box of red dye, we had pink shorts. The second box of dye produced pinker shorts. After three rounds of red dye, we had light, very light, red shorts. Despite the red jerseys and light red shorts, the big night was set to begin. The stands were full, the college president Cuyler Dunbar was in attendance, and even the local newspapers covered the game. After that game I never had to write my own newspaper articles again. We won the game by more than twenty points, and that night became the true coming-out party for the new CVCC program.

Following that game, I was suddenly able to recruit, and people actually knew that CVCC had a basketball team. We won seven more games to win the Western Tar Heel Conference regular season title. The following week we faced Surry Community College in the Western Tar Heel Conference tournament semifinals. We won by ten points. The next game was for the Western Tar Heel Conference championship. It was against rival Caldwell Community College, the same college I had played for sixteen years earlier. We jumped out to an early 11–0 lead and never looked back, winning the Western Tar Heel Conference title in our first season and finishing with twenty straight wins. Our lone loss was the season opener to Wilkes Community College.

Dale Wicker finished the season as our Most Valuable Player and the tournament MVP. Dale's own comeback story was in all of the local newspapers. He was even recruited by several four-year colleges. The story of a young man who could not make his high school team and two years later was a junior college most valuable player on a title winning team, what a comeback! Dale and his parents were very proud, and deservedly so. Dale went to a four-year college and received his degree.

After the season ended, I approached the college president about the possibility of CVCC joining the National Junior College Athletic Association the following year, so we could have an opportunity to win not only a Western Tar Heel Conference championship, but a national championship. Dunbar was very interested in the idea. At that time he was raising money through bonds to build a multipurpose facility that would include a gymnasium. Simultaneously, he was working on securing funds for a new science building for the college. The thought of having a gym and a weight room for the new basketball program was like a dream come true. While I knew it would be two years down the road, it would be worth waiting for.

President Dunbar presented the idea of joining the NJCAA to the college's Board of Directors, I spoke at the meeting, and the motion was approved. CVCC joined the NJCAA, the junior college "big time." While I was not aware of it, the board's decision did not please many of the older faculty members. They believed CVCC was a technical trade school and not a junior college. They felt that any available funds should be spent on academics and technical programs, not on athletics. When Catawba Valley Community College was founded in 1958, it was first known as Catawba Valley Technical Institute and then later as Catawba Valley Technical College. It was established with the goal and idea of helping students grow in the technical fields in order to enter the local work force. A large percentage of the faculty was still of this mindset.

Entering my second season, I began to recruit my first NJCAA team. The NJCAA announced that CVCC would play in NJCAA Region Ten. The region consisted of eight teams throughout North Carolina, South Carolina, and Georgia. As the season approached, I was excited about building a college program from scratch. I arranged for us to use Bandy's High School in Catawba for our practices and home games. Even though it was twenty miles away and we had to practice at 9:30 PM, due to the high school team's practices, it was still better than sharing the local recreation center. I sold season tickets to businesses and individuals to aid in paying for scholarships and brand new uniforms. The bottoms and tops actually matched! No pink shorts for us!

We opened our initial NJCAA season on November 1, 1992 at Spartanburg Methodist College, the number one ranked NJCAA team in the nation. This was not how I intended to start a new program or a new season. The CVCC athletic director had scheduled the game as a favor to his friend, the athletic director at Spartanburg Methodist. Our tallest player was six feet six inches tall; SMC had four players over seven feet tall. We kept the game close for the first half of the game, but lost by twenty. While disappointed, I realized all of the opponents we would face were not going to be as good as SMC.

As the season progressed, our team did much better than expected from a second year program. With the surprising success came calls and visits from college coaches nationwide. Duke University had never had a junior college player on its roster, yet their assistant coach, Tommy Amaker, contacted me regularly regarding our star player, Tony Florence. Thanks to Tony, the CVCC program was now on the NCAA map. I received telephone calls, letters, and visits from coaches who had been heroes of mine during my teen years. The *Hickory Daily Record* gave the team game by game front-page coverage. The CVCC athletic director, who was also the golf coach, commented to me several times that when his golf team won the NJCAA national championship, it was on the back page of the sports section. I understood his frustration, but I also knew that college basketball at any college is more popular than golf!

All of this positive publicity further enraged the faculty members, who by now had taken a strong stance against the CVCC president and the basketball program. Those faculty members continued to lobby for the science building over the multipurpose facility. From the first day I spoke to Dunbar, he indicated that there was a way to have both buildings if the faculty would be patient.

The CVCC regular season ended with a second straight Western Tar Heel Conference title, a runner-up finish in NJCAA Region Ten, and an 18–9 regular season record. The following week the Region Ten Tournament was held in Greenville, NC. The tournament consisted of an eight-team field. The winner advanced to the final sixteen in the nation. We defeated number six seed Lenior Community College in overtime. This set up a rubber match against Clinton Junior College. We had split during the regular season, with both teams capturing home victories. The game was tight throughout the first thirty minutes. With ten minutes to go, I called a timeout and instructed the team to play an offense we had not used all season. I placed four players on one side of the court. This allowed Tony Florence freedom to use the whole other side of the court. Our next seven possessions, Tony scored every way imaginable, from dunks and layups to three point shots. With five minutes to go we were up by twelve points and on our way to a twenty-four-point victory. CVCC had won its way into the NJCAA Region 10 championship game in its first season.

We faced the number two seed Aiken Tech, whom we had beaten twice during the regular season. We led the game throughout, but eventually lost the championship 67–66 on a thirty–five-foot last-second bank shot. That was a depressing moment for me, as I felt we had the best team and had been defeated by a lucky shot. I had no idea that this low point was insignificant compared to the curve ball that awaited me the following week.

After returning home from the tournament, I spent the next day reviewing the season and planning for the next one. While I was disappointed, we had had a very successful initial season, and I was excited about having seven players returning the following year. On Monday I arrived at the college and was met by three members of the *Hickory Daily Record*. I thought they were there to write a story about the success of our NJCAA program. Instead, they were there because an anonymous caller from the college had reported to the newspaper and to the NJCAA that CVCC had used academically ineligible players during the season.

I immediately left my office and met with the college president. He informed me that the athletic director, who was responsible for making sure students were eligible to play, had made several mistakes on the NJCAA eligibility forms. We had used players who were not academically qualified. This came as a great shock to me. The athletic director had filled out those forms for his golf team for over ten years and had never made a mistake. It was hard to believe that he had miscalculated four of my player's grades.

There was much speculation that this was all a ploy to have the president removed and the basketball team banished. The ploy worked. The following week, the Board of Directors disbanded the basketball program altogether. I was devastated. I had worked hard to build this new program, had followed the rules, and it had been taken away from me by political machinations from within. The two weeks that followed were tense and embarrassing. Everyone naturally thought that this was the work of a cheating coach. I heard that many times. In reality Dr. Louise Green, President of Student Services, wrote a letter of recommendation for me, applauding the job I had done as coach at CVCC. What others failed to realize was that I had no control or access to the NJCAA forms or the students' grades. I still wonder who was responsible for that embarrassing situation.

In early April I was informed that the Central Piedmont College coaching job was open. CPCC was a program with great potential. Central Piedmont College was the third largest junior college in the nation. Their basketball team had been placed on NJCAA probation numerous times for various violations. The college's athletic director was hoping to put the basketball program on the national map. I was one of nine coaches interviewed for the head coaching position. A week after the interview, I was offered and accepted the position. I was happy God had allowed me another comeback, leading me closer to my dream of becoming a NCAA coach. I also had the opportunity to resurrect another program and put it on the comeback trail.

Despite all the fighting from within and negative publicity that CVCC received, President Dunbar was able to save his job. He not only saved his job; he was able to orchestrate the completion of both the science building and the multipurpose facility as promised. In an unexpected comeback, CVCC resurrected its NJCAA basketball program in 2004, and a building was named in honor of the college president. Chalk up a big comeback for CVCC President Cuyler Dunbar and the CVCC basketball program. Today pictures of those first two teams proudly hang in the CVCC multipurpose facility.

The 1993-94 CVCC Bucs finished 20-8 in the first season of NJCAA play.

IX

I have learned to be content in any and every situation ... I can do everything through him who gives me strength. Philippians. 4:12–13

It was hard to understand why the series of events that led me to CPCC occurred. I just wanted to make sure history did not repeat itself. I knew I was lucky and blessed to have another shot at coaching college basketball . Being chosen from eight other candidates to head up the Central Piedmont basketball program was like a dream come true. I was coaching at the third largest junior college in the country, with an unlimited pool of talent, and with an on-campus gym.

I started my newest comeback in August 1994, when I began meeting returning players from Central Piedmont and recruiting players from CVCC's disbanded program. Central Piedmont's program needed a major comeback, and I believed I was the coach that could bring this team to national prominence. Central Piedmont had a bad reputation in Region 10 from always being in trouble and on probation. The three seasons prior to my arrival brought only embarrassment to the president, faculty, coaches, and players, due to NJCAA violations. My job was to turn this program into a winner, one the city, school administration, students, and players could be proud of.

I started out with a plan, which first and foremost included recruiting solid student athletes with good character. I wanted players who were talented enough to play at a Division I college, but needed help academically in order to qualify for a four-year school. A player a lot like myself when I graduated from East Lincoln in 1977. I was fortunate enough to have four CVCC players follow me to Central Piedmont, creating a solid foundation. I held open tryouts before the season started and found five more players. Six players returned from the previous season, so I started the season with fifteen players and a dream of a championship season. The first several weeks, I preached the "coming back" theme to my players, because I had players with bad experiences from the previous year—the transferring players because of the CVCC debacle, and the returning Central Piedmont players because of the previous season's troubles that had led to probation.

As the start of the 1994–95 season approached, I decided to write a book. The book was dedicated to God in appreciation for leading me from fast-food management to realizing my dream of coaching college basketball. The book was titled *Fast Food to Fast Breaks*.

Before the school term began in the fall of 1994, Houston Fancher, the head coach at North Greenville Junior College and now head coach at Appalachian State University, contacted me. Coach Fancher informed me that he had a player who had been dismissed from North Greenville for a minor infraction.. He told me this young man was from Lincolnton, my hometown, and his name was Aaron Grooms. I was familiar with him from following his successful high school career. Coach Fancher indicated that Aaron was a great kid who needed a fresh start. I contacted Aaron and his parents, and he decided to attend Central Piedmont and continue his education and basketball career.

The season went extremely well. Our team was invited to a holiday tournament in Jekyll Island, Georgia. We were the only Division Two college participating, as the other three teams were Division One. This meant that they had scholarships and living and dining facilities on campus. We faced the host team, Brunswick Community College, on the opening night. With three seconds to go in the game, CVCC transfer Cory Edwards hit a twenty-two-foot shot to win the game. The following evening we faced Florida Community College-Jacksonville, the nationally ranked number four college. We entered the game a huge underdog. Our team hit fourteen three-point shots that night, and we won the title going away. This tournament was one of many highlights from that initial season.

Another special moment came on the evening that we traveled to Chapel Hill, NC, to face the UNC Tar Heel's Junior Varsity team. I coached in the Dean Smith Center, and Central Piedmont defeated the Tar Heels by twenty points. After the game we were invited to stay for the UNC versus Maryland varsity game. It had already been a special time for me, just meeting Dean Smith and coaching in the Smith Center. Little did I know the special night was not over with.

After the varsity game we were locked in the hallway leading to the locker rooms. I asked a security guard what we were waiting for. He responded only by nodding his head and pointing toward the door. At that moment Michael Jordan and Antwan Jamison walked into the hallway. Jamison was on his official recruiting visit to UNC; Jordan had come along with him. My wife, children, team, and I were only an arm's length away from the greatest basketball player in the history of the game. My wife was so excited she said, "Michael it's you, it's really you!"

Both Jordan and Jamison were very personable. They talked to all of us and left the arena as we did. I noticed as we were leaving that Jamison was driving a beat-up car that smoked as he pulled out of the parking lot. We followed him to a service station. I jokingly told him that if he decided against UNC, he was welcome to play for me at Central Piedmont. Jamison went on to star at UNC and in the NBA. He no longer drives that beat-up car.

Central Piedmont finished the season with twenty-one wins and ten losses. We won the NJCAA Region Ten regular season title, but suffered a season-ending loss in the semifinals of the NJCAA Region 10 Tournament. From this team Aaron Grooms received a basketball scholarship to Wingate University. Cory Edwards received a scholarship to Lees McRae College, and Rodney Gidney received a scholarship to Livingstone College. All three would play two more years of college basketball and receive their four- year degrees. These men completed their own comebacks. Together, the players and I were able to come back and have a positive experience. Our team received front-page coverage from the *Charlotte Observer* sports columnist Tom Sorenson, radio coverage, coverage from national magazines, and a top ten national ranking.

Following my initial season, I received a verbal contract extension for the following 1995–96 season by the athletic director and his supervisor. The contract extension was announced at the Central Piedmont basketball banquet in May, with players, parents, students, and new recruits in attendance. I recruited fourteen new players that I believed would catapult the school into national prominence. The fourteen players included two seven footers. It was such a strong recruiting class that Dick Vitale's pre-season college basketball publication rated Central Piedmont as one of the top five junior college teams in the country. A writer from the magazine called me requesting information for a story he wanted to write about the quick rise of Central Piedmont's basketball program. I forwarded the request to the athletic director, who told me that he needed permission from Central Piedmont's president.

In June a high school coach from Gastonia, NC, telephoned me at my home to inquire about the possibility of my recruiting one of his departing seniors. The coach indicated the player was a good defensive player and an overall average high school player. I told the coach that I would take a look at him, but explained that the best-case scenario would be for his player to redshirt in 1995 and try out for the team in 1996. Redshirting would mean he could practice with the team but not play in any games. This would allow the young man to gain valuable practice experience without sacrificing a year of eligibility. The following Saturday I met with the player and watched him work out. I knew he would never make my college team or any other college team. He seemed like a good kid, but just did not have the talent to play at the college level. I explained to him that he could be a manager, film person, or statistics keeper.

Two months later on August 7, 1994, the Central Piedmont athletic director informed me that I was to attend the NJCAA Region Ten meeting in Greensboro, NC. On August 10, I attended the meeting. At the yearly meeting, region basketball schedules were set, new rules were announced and explained, and a region director was elected. Despite only three seasons of NJCAA coaching experience, my peers elected me to be the Region Ten director.

One week later the AD telephoned me and inquired about the player from Gastonia that I had agreed could serve as a team manager. I told the AD that the young man's coach had asked me to take a look at the player and that I had done so. I also informed him that the young man did not have the talent or potential to play at the college level. The AD then informed me that this student had gone to the financial aid office and told them that I'd given him a scholarship to play basketball. Being a NJCAA Division III college, we had no athletic scholarships. The only financial aid available was the same for any other student, which included grants, loans, and Pell Grants. I explained to the AD that what the young man was saying was not true.

That night the young man's sister called me to find out why her brother was not getting a basketball scholarship. I explained the situation in detail to her. The following morning I received a third call from the Central Piedmont AD stating that a mother from Newton, NC, had written a letter to him. The letter stated that I had recruited her son Mark and that he did not have anywhere to live in Charlotte. She believed it was my fault. She further stated in the letter that I had destroyed the Catawba Valley Community College program while coaching there, and had been fired from the head coaching position. Due to my actions, she continued, Catawba Valley Community College had been forced to disband their basketball program.

Aside from the fact that none of that was true, I did not recruit her son to play for Central Piedmont. He was a below average player. He was, however, a friend of a player that I was recruiting from the same own. The player I was recruiting did not have a car, so his friend had driven him to Charlotte to tour our campus. While there, the friend asked me if he could try out for the team. I explained to him that we conducted open tryouts for every student, and tryouts were conducted a week before official practice began. I told him he was welcome to attend, and that ended our conversation.

I explained all of this to the AD, and faxed him my letter of recommendation from Catawba Valley Community College, providing proof that the mother's statements about me were fabricated. On August 21, the AD arranged a meeting with my assistant coach and me. We were both quizzed about our recruiting methods. The AD was interested in knowing how we recruited such a great team with no financial aid and no on-campus housing.

I told him that our biggest tool were letters sent from NCAA coaches to my former players. This was the recruiting tool that I had mentioned to Tom Sorenson, the sportswriter, when he asked the same question. I had created a notebook containing letters from most of the major college programs from across the country. The letters were a huge selling tool. Every NJCAA player dreamed of playing Division One college basketball, and the letters allowed the recruits to see that we had great connections at the Division I level.

My assistant coach and I also helped the players by completing applications for Pell Grants and other forms of financial aid. This aid gave the players a means of support. We also had connections at several area facilities that provided part-time jobs for the players, or work-study jobs. I further explained to the AD that I tried to make our schedule very desirable for the incoming student athlete. I scheduled tournaments in Florida, Jekyll Island, along the coast of North Carolina, and games against Division One junior varsity teams. The schedule included playing the UNC junior varsity team, and we were given tickets to the varsity game that followed our game. I believed we were giving these kids a chance to live a dream, and get an education.

After we'd answered his questions, the AD informed us that the college president did not want Dick Vitale's magazine or any other magazine on campus to cover the team. He said that even if we won the NJCAA national championship and every player was given a scholarship to a four-year college, the program would not have the president's support. The president had stated that more college presidents were fired over athletics than any other reason.

I left the meeting stunned. I thought I'd been hired to win games and produce good student athletes. Four days later the AD telephoned me at home. He informed me that he had decided not to renew my contract and that if I had anything belonging to the college, to return it. I was shocked beyond belief. I could not believe that I had had two college coaching opportunities, and circumstances beyond my control had caused me to lose both positions. This was another example of the actions of one person controlling another person's life. I asked God why this had happened to me. I had coached for three seasons, won at least twenty games every season, produced students that went on to four-year colleges, and had won a championship every season that I coached. Why had this happened? The following afternoon, my granddaddy Coffey passed away. Talk about a bad week.

I was forced to call my fellow Region Ten coaches and tell them that I had been terminated and had to give up my position of Region Ten director. After I'd made over one hundred phone calls to the Central Piedmont's president's office and the AD's office, I was told I could meet with a college administrator. I attended the meeting expecting to be able to tell my side of the story and find out why I had been terminated. The person with whom I met only knew my name and was not even aware of the purpose of our meeting. At the end of the meeting he told me he would review the situation and I would hear from his office within a week. Sixteen years later, I still have not heard from him.

The day after the meeting I called the AD to inquire as to when I could clean out my office. I called him for the next eleven days before I was told there was nothing in my office. In fact, I had had a collection of books, tapes, letters, autographs, and pictures in my office. Still I was told nothing in the office belonged to me. The following morning I hired an attorney from Lincolnton to pursue obtaining of my belongings.

The next week I received calls from parents and players concerned about me and about the firing. They had been told that I'd been fired for telling potential student athletes that I would give them scholarships to play basketball. They were also told that I had not disclosed my firing from CVCC, which was not true. I spoke to the fourteen players I had recruited, and they all agreed that I had not told them they would receive a scholarship. I informed my attorney of this information, and he decided we should file a defamation of character suit.

Six months later, my deposition was taken by the Central Piedmont attorneys. After the deposition was completed, the stenographer told my attorney that we had a great case. Her positive statement encouraged me. The following month I paid for a copy of the deposition. One year later, a trial date was set. The evening before the trial was to begin I contacted my attorney to ask if I needed to bring anything, and what witnesses should be on call. My attorney informed me that he had requested a dismissal since he had not received my deposition. I asked why the deposition had not been ordered. He said the deposition had been ordered, but had been misplaced by his staff. I contacted the stenographer, and she stated that my attorney never ordered the deposition.

Over the next year I contacted my attorney's office more than two hundred times, trying to find out the status of my case. Several times I was told that the case had been re-filed. When I spoke to the clerk of court, she informed me that the case was never re-filed. Exactly one year later, on the last day to re-file the lawsuit, I went to the attorney's office and forced him to re-file the case that same afternoon.

Another year passed, and a court date was finally set. I appeared in court with my attorney. Six cases were scheduled to be heard before mine. My attorney informed me that it would be three or four days before my case was heard. He suggested I leave, and that he would call me in time to get there for the hearing. The next day my attorney informed me that the case had been called the previous day, after I had left. He had presented the evidence and the judge had dismissed the case. I asked him why he hadn't called me, why our witnesses were not there, and why the deposition was never presented. He had no answer. After five years of waiting I did not get my belongings, nor was I able to clear my name publicly.

The following day I collected my file from the attorney's office. Originally, my mindset was that there was no coming back from this experience. There was nothing to be profited from this event. I had been dismissed for situations I had had no control over, and five years later, I had lost the opportunity to clear my name and receive what was rightfully mine. I knew I had a winnable case, but due to the actions of my attorney, my case was never presented. As far as anyone knew, I had been fired from my jobs at Catawba Valley Community College and at Central Piedmont Community College for violations. I would never coach college basketball again.

I was wrong in my assumption that nothing positive could come from these back-to-back events in my life. I realize now that these events and others like them were not acts of God against us. While I was devastated and disappointed, I did not blame God for this happening to me. In the past I would have questioned God and his motives. Instead, I thanked God for allowing me those three years of coaching. I made a decision to change my outlook, quit feeling sorry for myself, and come back from the sweeping curve ball life had thrown at me. I knew that I needed a change and a new set of goals. It would be easy to wallow in my sorrow and cry about my misfortunes, but his was not God's wish for me. He wanted me to hit this curveball out of the park.

The 1994-95 Central Piedmont Community College team finished as the Region X regular season champions and a top 10 national ranking.

In everything you do, put God first, and he will direct
you and crown your effort with success. Proverbs 3:6

When men reach their midforties, they supposedly go through a second childhood or midlife crisis. Some men buy fancy sports cars, date younger women, or try new hobbies or careers. Me? All I wanted to do was to play college basketball again! I realize it's a strange dream to have at age forty-four, but by July 2003, I decided that I had dreamed about playing college basketball for long enough. I was going to quit thinking about it and do something about it.

I wrote to the NJCAA to inquire about my eligibility status. I guess they thought it was a joke and never answered any of my four inquiries. I then e-mailed Coach Bill Payne at Caldwell Community College. My theory was that Caldwell Community College was where I had started my college career in 1977, and it was where I wanted to finish it in 2004. My e-mail began, "This may be the weirdest letter you have ever received."

I told Coach Payne of my past at Caldwell, about my coaching experiences, and of my desire to come back and play college basketball. To my surprise, he was all for it. He invited me to a workout on the following Saturday. I showed up for the tryout as a forty-four-year-old man with a dream. I left with the respect of everyone in attendance, including the coach. As I walked off the court I asked Coach Payne, "Not bad for a forty-four-year-old?" He laughed and replied, "Not bad for a twenty-year-old!"

In August I registered for classes, and thus began my final year of college basketball. I was finally going to realize my dream of playing again. After twenty-eight years, I returned to college basketball. I did not know that a month later this dream would once again have to be put on hold, maybe forever. Following the first week of pre-season workouts, our youngest daughter Taren was a passenger in an automobile accident that claimed the life of one of her friends. This accident changed my entire outlook on life. I withdrew from college and tried to help Anna Marie in assisting Taren through this very difficult period. She withdrew from high school, and we homeschooled her for the remainder of the school year.

I stayed in touch with Coach Payne and the team during the season. The team won the Western Tar Heel Conference and the Region Ten Tournament, advancing to the NJCAA National Tournament in New York. In the first round, Caldwell was slotted to play Joliet Junior College, a school from the same area Anna Marie hails from. At the time of the national tournament, we were visiting her parents. I had the opportunity to see Joliet JC play twice. I took notes and called Coach Payne with an in-depth scouting report the day before the two teams met. The next morning I woke up and read the Joliet newspaper headlines: "Caldwell defeats Joliet." I was happy to have played a small part in a national tournament victory.

The following summer our son Jeremy made the decision to attend Caldwell to complete his two-year degree. With the help of friends and family and their many prayers, Taren made her own terrific comeback and was now prepared to return to high school. She has since graduated from high school and is currently in her final year of college studying to be an elementary special educationb teacher. Taren's comeback has made it possible for me to reconsider my own comeback once again.

XI

In everything you do, put God first, and he will direct you and crown your effort with success. Proverbs 3:6

Jeremy and I attended all of the Caldwell summer practices together, and I started thinking of the possibility of playing college basketball on the same team as my son. Jeremy was also making his own personal comeback. He had been an excellent high school athlete, and was a starter on the football and basketball teams. He received recruiting letters from several major colleges, including Dartmouth and Virginia Tech. The third football game of his senior year, he was injured on a late hit that severely tore his ACL. The following week he had surgery and was unable to play any sports for over a year. The injury was hard for all of us to cope with, but with God's help, we managed to make the best of the situation. We were very proud of Jeremy because he never let the injury or the loss of his senior seasons effect him. He remained positive throughout the year.

Two years passed before Jeremy was ready to come back and try his hand at playing college basketball. I am still amazed at how this opportunity developed. So many events and situations had to balance out for this dream to become reality. I was not sure how Jeremy felt about playing on a team with his forty-fiveyear old Dad but from the first time I mentioned the idea, he was thrilled. I knew it was going to be a wonderful experience, but I also knew it would be no easy task. That would turn out to be an understatement.

Saturday, June 19, 2004: Jeremy and I attended the Caldwell practice today. I am just testing the waters to see if I can be an asset to this year's team. The scrimmage went well. There were twenty players there. I did not have a good day because I was tired from the outset. Running a distance is not the same as running sprints. Jeremy played very well and made a good impression.

Saturday, July 17, 2004: Jeremy and I went to the Caldwell practice today. Jeremy played solid again and I had a much better day than last month. Coach Payne also thought I had a good day. I still have not decided if I can make this year's team. We had twenty players again, and only fifteen will make the squad.

Tuesday, August 14, 2004: I did it! I took the first step in making my COMEBACK attempt. I registered for classes today at Caldwell Community College. Jeremy also registered. If I do decide to go out for the team, Jeremy and I will be playing together, on the same college basketball team. Jeremy and I are undefeated on our driveway over a ten-year period, so I think we make good teammates!

Wednesday, September 22, 2004: The first day of tryouts at Caldwell. I am beat. I am in shape for my age, but man those young guys can get up and down the floor. There are actually three players trying out that are in worse shape than I am. A total of twenty-one players are vying for fifteen positions. Coach Payne will name the team on October 8th.

Thursday, September 23, 2004: Practice went really well for me and Jeremy. Two players did not show today. We are now down to nineteen. I am very sore and tired, but pleased with my progress and energy.

Friday, September 24, 2004: I managed to get through week one of tryouts. I pulled a hamstring today but I hope it is nothing serious. We were running sprints, for me that's still not very fast, and my hamstring pulled. I finished practice but was even slower than usual. It was not a good day. Still nineteen players, so there will be four players cut. I think I have a good chance of making the team as I have played well up until the injury. I also think I can bring leadership to this team.

Tuesday, September 28, 2004: We had a three-day break and I hoped that the break would give my leg time to heal. Instead I pulled the other hamstring at tryouts today. I continued to practice, but it is getting harder and harder to move. I want to move my legs but just can't do it. I still hope to make the team, but I have to get well or I will be of no benefit to the Cobra squad.

Friday, October 1, 2004: I have now practiced for two weeks with torn hamstrings and now a sore calf muscle. I think I may have waited a year or two too long to try this COMEBACK. My body just won't allow this kind of daily physical stress anymore. If it was regular season practice and game minutes, I could do it. Preseason practice is a different story. This is like boot camp. I know why his name is Payne now more than ever.

Saturday, October 2, 2004: Went to practice. Started going through the drills but the pain was too severe, so I sat out most of practice. I am very disappointed. I know God wants me to make this COMEBACK, yet I get sidetracked at every turn.

Monday, October 4, 2004: More of the same. I tried to go through practice, but I was so slow that I was way behind on every drill. Coach Payne finally told me to sit down if I could not go at full speed. I wanted to but there was no way.

Tuesday, October 5, 2004: Went to practice. Made it through

the entire practice in agony, but made it. When I walked in the house tonight, Anna Marie and her mother, the best mother-in-law in the universe, looked at the backs of my legs and gasped, because my hamstrings are black, blue, and purple. I know now that the dream of coming back has come to an end. I called Coach Payne at his home and informed him that I would not be able to play this season. He was disappointed but understood. It is a really sad day for me. This is something I have dreamed of for over twenty years and now it is over. I can honestly say that I gave it 100 percent. I do not question God, as his will is my will. Maybe this was just my dream and not a mission.

But those who hope in the Lord will renew their strength. They will soar on wings like eagles, they will run and not grow weary, they will walk and not be faint. Isaiah 40:31

While pursuing my dream of becoming the world's oldest college basketball player, I was still working fulltime in the commercial cleaning business. How I ended up in this business is one question I'll have to ask God when we meet. I know that when the teachers in school asked me what I wanted to be when I grew up, I didn't say "janitor." However, I guess I really was destined for this trade. In the fifth grade I mopped the cafeteria floor at Iron Station School for a soda. Hey, it was a sixteen-ounce Pepsi! In my eighth grade year, I helped my dad in his job as janitor at the local Baptist church. As I see it now, this was my destiny.

While learning the commercial cleaning trade in my early years, I worked for a janitorial franchise company. I benefited from the training and educational tools that the company offered. They paid for my education at the Cleaning Management Institute. During this same time I completed my Registered Building Service Manager training and became one of only two hundred and fifty RBSMs nationwide. I benefited the franchise company by being a motivated operations manager. Over a three-year period I oversaw a huge comeback within our operations department. Our customer loss percentage dropped from a national worst of 5.5 % to a national best of 1.89%. I was responsible for over two hundred accounts in seven counties. A fifty- to sixty-hour workweek was common. I was willing to do whatever it took to help the company come back from being the nation's worst to the best, and I was successful in doing so.

While I was very appreciative for the training and experience the company gave me, it also provided me with a lesson I was not expecting. It was a lesson of selfishness and greed. I witnessed firsthand how owners and upper management of companies paid workers minimal amounts while they became extremely wealthy. While their words sounded good, the truth of the matter was that upper management was the only one making money. At the annual awards banquet, the Franchisee of the Year was announced. The two-time winner told me she didn't have enough money that evening to buy even one drink. She was the Franchisee of the Year! I eventually resigned from my position, because I could not witness and be a party to this injustice year after year. I had been thinking about getting involved in the sales area of commercial cleaning and saw this as my opportunity to set new goals and learn a new area of the business.

After my resignation I enjoyed great success selling new commercial cleaning contracts for other companies. Over the seven years that followed, I sold over nine million square feet in new business, resulting in 3.6 million dollars in yearly revenue. The success that I have achieved is all based on Christian principles, including a lack of debt, fair treatment of employees and customers, and simply being kind to others. "Do unto others as you would have them do unto you."

While I have many business success stories, I have experienced bad days as well. Recently I lost a million-dollar contract. This was an account I had worked three years to obtain. The business was not lost due to poor performance issues, but because of underhanded business dealings by people I had once considered friends. Not only were they friends, but friends that I had encouraged to open their own business.

Was this a bad day? No. It was a very disappointing event, but not a bad day. I could still look to the sky, see the sunshine, hear the birds sing, and ask the Lord for his will to be done. I asked God to help me replace the business if that was his will. I started working toward a goal, and have now had a comeback with one new account that more than replaces what I lost. I was happy about this business comeback, but if I had not replaced the business, it would not affect my happiness or my outlook on life. Why should it? If today was my last day, would that account really matter?

No business, no matter how large or small, can be successful spending more revenue than it generates. No individual, business, city, county, or nation can be successful if it spends more money than it makes. Our country needs to come back not only as I mentioned before to moral values, but to economical values as well. Bring jobs back to our country. Quit paying people to have babies and remain unemployed. Quit spending $450 on a $10 tool.

In July 2009 the United States unemployment rate was at 9.4%, the highest since 1950. The United States total national debt has increased over $5 billion every year since 2003. In 2008 the national budget increased by $1 trillion, the first time in history that level had been reached. While we look around and see that these facts are true, our government continues to spend dollars we don't have. It is not only spending that money, but wasting it. The federal government cannot account for $24.5 billion spent in 2003. A recent White House review of the federal budget indentified $90 billion spent on programs that were ineffective or operating under a flawed purpose.

This system is not working and will never work until we as individuals and as a nation understand this simple concept. Why do people go into debt for things they cannot afford, just for appearance's sake? Not many decades ago there was no credit except at the general store, and even when credit was available, the older generations knew better than to go into debt. They lived on what money they made and found ways to be happy, even though they may not have had the fanciest, largest, or most modern possessions. We as individuals need to return to accumulating minimal debt based not on our current situations, but taking into consideration the possibility of job loss, injury, or other unforeseen circumstance. The results of our not learning from these mistakes are that between March 2008 and March 2009, over 1.5 million United States citizens filed for bankruptcy. Lesson learned? I doubt it!

The same goes for any business. In our business, as owners, we would rather work sixteen- and seventeen-hour days on a new account than pay employees to work and go into debt. Once the account is at an acceptable profit margin, we hire and train employees. This is just one of the methods we have used to become successful business owners. These methods not only apply to our business, but can apply to any business of any size. I fail to understand why large corporations reward CEOs with millions of dollars in bonuses for doing a good job. Is that not why they were hired and what they are expected to do? Businesses should give bonuses to the employees actually laboring in the field. By giving bonuses to the upper management, corporations send a message to the lower ranks that they are not as important or deserving.

This causes morale problems, affecting the quality of work from employees. The lack of quality products, services, and just plain bad business sense can destroy any business in a short period of time. Individuals, businesses, counties, cities, and countries all should follow the same methods of operations, with the bottom line being: treat everyone fairly and spend less money than you generate.

While working full-time, attending college full-time, and playing basketball consumed a large amount of my time, I still made business my top priority. I made sure that every one of our customers remained happy, every employee was treated fairly, and I continued selling new business at a record pace. After failing in my quest to come back to Caldwell Community College and play basketball, I had much more time to spend on business. While I enjoyed the free time, I missed basketball and missed my last chance to come back ... or so I thought.

Me with Mr. Clean on my way to becoming one of
the top sales producers in the nation

November 2, 2004: Caldwell opened the season at tough Spartanburg Methodist. Caldwell lost by twenty points. It was Jeremy's first college game. He led the team with five rebounds.

November 13, 2004: Caldwell was defeated by New River Community College today. The loss ended a three-game winning streak. It was a game we should have won by forty. We just don't play together. There is no leadership. My legs are finally feeling better.

December 5, 2004: Caldwell defeated Truett McConnell College today. It was great to get a win. We still did not play together as a team. Everybody wants to be a scorer instead of each player doing his part to win the game. We are now 6–7 on the season. All of the players are down. I sat in the stands and can't believe this team is playing this poorly. With Coach Payne, it's only a matter of time before he brings out the best in this team.

Christmas Tournament: Lost to rival Catawba Valley Community College in the championship game. We played no defense. I wish I were playing. I think I could help bring a winning attitude to this team. We are entering Christmas break with a losing 7–8 record. This team is much better than the record indicates.

December 28, 2004: I received a call from Coach Payne today. He wants to meet with me tomorrow. I think he may want me to help with practices or scout opponents.

December 29, 2004: I can't believe it! Unbelievable! Coach Payne wants me to join the team. There are several players that are ineligible due to their grades. He needs a tenth player so they can scrimmage at practice. Coach Payne asked if I was ready to suit up. I replied "Sure." The dream and the COMEBACK are alive. I worked out with the team today and all went well.

January 3, 2005 Made it through an entire practice. My hamstring cramped one time and I just told God that this was his call. It does not seem to be re-injured.

Thursday, January 6, 2005: Made it through another practice with no injuries. I am very excited. I am going on a road trip this weekend. Jeremy and I will play our first college basketball together on the same court.

Friday, January 7, 2005: Played in my first college game in twenty-eight years. We defeated Sampson CC 83–72. I scored two points and had two rebounds. Playing on the same team as Jeremy is a great experience. The COMEBACK is complete. I played! It is strange rooming with a teenage teammate. He's interested in picking up girls; I'm interested in watching *Sports Center* and going to bed.

Saturday, January 8, 2005: We won again. We defeated Central Carolina 81–73 to even our record at 9–9. Two wins in two days. I can already see a difference in attitude.

January 10, 2005: Revenge. We defeated Catawba Valley Community College 103–84. I played terribly. I did not look forty-six, I looked seventy-six. No points and one rebound, but we won. We are now 10–9 and 3–0 PGE (Post Grandpa ERA).

Thursday, January 13, 2005: Four in a row! We defeated 10th ranked Oxford, GA, 64–60. Oxford was ranked number ten in the latest NJCAA national rankings. Before the game the Oxford players were laughing at me. After I scored on an offensive rebound to preserve our lead late in the game, the Oxford coach yelled to his players, "Who's laughing now?" After the game the Oxford coach congratulated me and told me what a big basket I made.

Saturday, January 15, 2005: We defeated Forsyth Tech today. My best game yet with four points and three rebounds. We have won five straight games. This is the longest winning streak of the season.

Wednesday, January 19, 2005: Make it six straight! We traveled to Mayland and defeated them 92–59. Five points and six rebounds, I'll take it.

January 26, 2005: Defeated Catawba Valley Community College. My parents came to the game! It was like old times. We are now 8–0 Post Grandpa Era. This team has really come together. It is a totally different attitude from early in the season. John Mark Brooks, the sports editor for the *Lincoln Times*, called me today. He conducted an interview with me for an upcoming article. I explained to him that this COMEBACK was a miracle, a gift from God. My hope is that just one person will read the article and be influenced in a positive manner. I really believe this was God's reason for allowing me to complete this comeback.

January 28, 2005: The article came out and it was great. There was a quarter page picture of Jeremy and me. I am very pleased with the article and think John did a great job of conveying the right message. The article was titled "Caldwell Cobras Truly a Family Affair." John wrote,

> This wasn't the way Jeff Coffey thought his life would turn out. His dream was to play professional basketball, but through a series of events and divine intervention, his plan changed. Now a far greater dream is being realized at Caldwell Community College. Jeff and his son Jeremy, a 2002 graduate from Bandy's High School, play on the Cobras, which are the No. 12 team in the country

with a 15–9 record. At 6'4" in 1977, with gifted athleticism and a feathery touch, Jeff racked up accolades as easily as he racked up points. He was a High School All-America as a senior on a team that included "Big Game" James Worthy, then at Ashbrook, and Sleepy Floyd at Hunter Huss. A First Team All-Gaston Gazette selection and All-Southern District 7 nod followed for Jeff who was Mustang Co-MVP with Lewis

"Re-C" Lowery, one of his best friends. Coffey averaged 17.3 points per game for his prep career. As a senior, he averaged a double-double with 18 points and 12 rebounds. Wake Forest and NC State recruited him, but at the time the requirement was having two foreign languages. Coffey did not have those, so he chose to attend Caldwell where he averaged 21 points per game as a freshman. After such a successful freshmen season, he left the school and tried his hand at the NBA. Coffey bounced around pro-am leagues and was invited to work out for the Washington Bullets NBA team in 1982. Still with the desire to play basketball he attempted to make the CBA and World Basketball League in 1988. Jeremy, Jeff's twenty-year-old son, was recruited by Dartmouth and Virginia Tech, but a torn ACL scared some recruiters off. As a result he decided to sign with Caldwell. Jeff was enrolled in four classes at the time of his son's signing. He would often work out with the team just to scratch his basketball itch. That's when opportunity and fate met. Caldwell lost three players for failing to meet Caldwell's academic requirements. Cobra's head coach Bill Payne asked Jeff if he was ready to join the team. "I told him sure," Jeff said. He's not the same player he was in 1978 but Jeff is averaging two points and two rebounds per game. More important are his intangibles, such as knowledge of the game and leadership. Since Jeff joined the team at Christmas break, Caldwell has gone 8–0, having started the season at 7–9. Jeremy believes the win streak is no coincidence. "He brings major leadership. He's always vocal, always gets us pumped. Just him being on the floor; he really doesn't have to say anything. He's just a natural-born leader." Wednesday night, Pat and C.E., Jeff's parents and Jeremy's grandparents, and wife Anna watched Jeff and Jeremy play against Catawba Valley, whom they beat 101–78. "It was, in a way, a thrill just to have them there. It was sort of sad, because I couldn't do the things that I used to do," Jeff said. Even though his son is just a shadow, on the court, of what he once was, his father was proud nonetheless. "I think it's wonderful. Jeff has always been such a basketball fanatic and he just can't give the sport up. He's played in the industrial leagues the last few years, so this was his opportunity to go back and play organized ball," C.E. said. "It's totally different, but I tell you what … there is nothing like playing on the same team as your son," Jeff said. His son agrees. "It's fun and I never thought I would ever be able to play on the same team with my dad. It's a new experience and I like it," said Jeremy, who averages three points a game, two rebounds and two assists. Some young men would be embarrassed by their dad suiting up beside them, but not Jeremy. "I welcomed it with open arms. Maybe some kids would have a problem with it, but I thought it was awesome. Especially being on the same court at the same time, passing each other the ball," he said. Jeremy views it as a blessing and knows just how fortunate he is. "Most 45-year-olds struggle playing pick-up ball and my dad is out there running with 19- and 20-year-old kids and playing just as hard," he said. Basketball teams are often said to be a family. Two of the Cobras are just that, pun intended. "All my teammates love having him out there. They tell me, 'I wish my pop was out there.'" Perhaps, just as special as the two being teammates on a college team, is the fact both the father and son seem to relish the opportunity and are proud of each other. "I'm very proud of him (Jeremy), not only because he's a good player, but because he's a good Christian boy. I'm proud of him that he is able to play at this level and I think he can go on to play at a four-year school."

February 5, 2005: What a game. My wife Anna, my children, my two grandchildren, former school friends, and my parents were all in attendance tonight. I had my best game of the year. I finished the night with six points, four rebounds, a blocked shot, and two assists, both to Jeremy. I could not have written a better script for this evening. Now even the home crowd is getting into the Grandpa era. They shout "Grandpa, Grandpa" when I enter the games.

February 6, 2005: We beat New River by 40 points. We lost to them before Christmas. This was a good gauge of how far this team has come.

February 11, 2005: We defeated Central Carolina tonight to clinch the Tar Heel conference regular season title. Our record stands at 18–10 and 11–0 NJCAA since I joined the team. We are now preparing for the Region 10 tournament. The winner will be one step away from the NJCAA National tournament in New York.

February 25, 2005: We defeated Mayland Community College in the Region 10 semifinals. We will now be facing Oxford for the title tomorrow. I feel good about tomorrow as it's my birthday.

February 26, 2005: I am forty-six years old today, and I suited up for the NJCAA Region Ten championship game. We lost to Oxford College 67–64, and thus my college basketball career has come to an end. The COMEBACK is now complete. God brought me the long way around but blessed me by allowing me to play college basketball. He also allowed me to play on the same team with my son Jeremy. I have heard of many instances in which a father coached a son. I have never heard of a father and son playing together on a college team. It was a wonderful, memorable experience. The end of the season is very sad for me. I dreamed of playing in the NJCAA National Tournament with my son Jeremy.

I see this comeback as a gift from God. For all of these events to present themselves in a manner that would lead me to finally realize my dream of playing college basketball, and being blessed to play on the same team as my son, was a gift that I will never forget.

March 2005: I was awarded the Courage Award at the basketball banquet. I was in Chicago and unable to attend, so Jeremy accepted the award on my behalf. It was only fitting that he accept in my place. My COMEBACK is complete. I hoped it would end with a national title, but most important, I have completed my mission. I am now presented with how to touch more people and help them to trust God through the good times, the bad times, and the comebacks through my own experiences. Maybe write a boo

The comeback is complete. Pictured are me and my team mates at Caldwell Community College.

XII

But the Lord said...I don't make decisions the way you do! Men judge by outward appearance, but I look at a man's thoughts and intentions. I Samual 16:7

Earlier I stated that everyone and every nation face struggles, problems, and tough situations. How individuals come back from these trials determines their happiness and the effects they will have on those around them and on their country. No one's life, and no country, is going to be without these trials. As a nation we better start over and take a hard look at what put us in the situation we are now facing. The United States is in its worst condition ever, in every area! Financially, educationally, morally, we are at an all-time low. Could it be because we have removed God and prayer from schools and every other public entity?

I don't believe our country is being punished by God for this. We are punishing ourselves by failing to live under the rules our forefathers set, based on Christian principles. While there has always been a separation of religion and state, the principles remain the same. We have to come back to those ways! It all has to start on an individual basis. We have to make sure the people we vote into office don't want to send all of our jobs overseas; or pay people more to sit at home than they can earn working; or that they don't believe in letting convicted criminals roam the streets with no fear of repercussion. That's just a start! We the people of the United States in order to form a more perfect union needs to take our country back. Back from rich politicians that have driven all of us into the pitiful state we are in today.

Before we can change our nation, though, we must change on an individual level. I look at my life, my family's lives, my friend's lives, and even the lives of those strangers I discussed earlier, and one thing is certain. Everyone has troubles. From the stories I've told of my past, it's easy to see that I was not exempt from trials, tribulations, and curve balls. How did I endure? I didn't do it alone. I did it with help from friends, family, and faith that God would give me the strength to overcome any adversity that arose. Knowing that God is always with us is the first step in coming back from even the worst situations and events. When we realize that God is with us, every second of every day, that lends each of us comfort and strength in all of life's situations.

Let's take a hard look at this life. Why worry about anything? How much good has worrying ever done? What has worrying ever changed? Not one single thing has been accomplished through worry. The worst that can happen to a person is to lose his or her life or the life of a loved one. That's the very worst! It's inconsequential if death occurs because of a long-term illness, an accident, a crime, or a tragic event such as 9/11. The loss of a life is sad for those left here on earth, but for a Christian, heaven is the ultimate reward for the life lived here.

Some people live difficult lives each and every day. There is no promise that things will ever improve. During the recent recession, I think we have all seen examples of this more than ever. While there is hope, there is no guarantee. Knowing that the greatest reward of all awaits us after this short life should bring us all comfort. If the worst that can happen to a person in a day is returning to God and seeing loved ones that had passed on before us, it's not going to be a bad day at all. Knowing that death in this life is the worst-case scenario, the rest is a breeze for me. When we realize that problems are always going to arise in every area of our lives, then we learn how to come back from these curve balls, and the happier we are.

How many times have you heard someone make the statement, "Every time I have any extra money, something bad happens and I lose everything I have. The car breaks down, the washing machine goes on the blink, the kid's college tuition is due. I can never get ahead!" I have heard it said many times. In God's big scheme of life, this or any other problem is not as important as the type of life we live, the way we treat others, and our response to adversity.

As I read the obituaries and watch the evening news, I see the deaths of many famous, notable, and wealthy people. I find myself wondering, "Where will they spend eternity?" We will, without fail, leave this earth with the same thing we came into it with— nothing. Of course we want to live as comfortably as possible, and allow our family to live as comfortably as possible. I have heard many Christians and non-Christians alike say that all we leave behind is our legacy. While this is true, even our legacy fades after a few generations. Think now … can you name ten people from the fifteenth century ? How about ten from the seventeenth?? That's how fast each of us is forgotten, no matter how rich or how famous we become! There is nothing wrong with having goals and wanting to be successful.

We all want to be successful. We want our families to get along well and our children to grow up to become perfect adults. We want world peace and zero crime. The world has never been able to achieve these goals and never will. We as individuals and as nations all falter and fall short of the glory of God many times over a lifetime. Once again, everyone is allowed to make his own decisions, and Satan can influence many of these decisions. I am interested in the lives and beliefs of the rich and famous, Donald Trump, Michael Jordan, Ted Turner, Oprah, Tiger Woods, and others of their stature and wealth. I wonder if they know and trust God, if they led their children and others to God, or if they have found their treasure on earth and missed out on the really important things in life. The Bible does say that it's easier for a camel to pass through the eye of a needle than for a rich man to enter the kingdom of God. Why is this? Does wealth corrupt the mind and the soul? Once a person passes from this world, wealth has no bearing.

On a recent episode of the popular Donald Trump show *The Apprentice*, the winning team was awarded a dinner with Mr. Trump's children. During the dinner, the participants were allowed to question the Trump children. All of the questions and answers were geared toward wealth, personality, and business advice. My first question would have been "Does he know God? Did he teach you about God?" If not, he is a failure and has failed his children. It is possible to be very poor and very happy. It is also possible to be very rich and very unhappy. Not only do worldly possessions and success not get a person to Heaven; wealth does not even guarantee happiness on earth. How many wealthy actors, musicians, and athletes have overdosed on drugs accidentally or as a means of suicide? If you want to be happy, know where you're going to spend eternity.

If a person lives to be a hundred years old, it's still a short time spent on earth. If a person makes millions of dollars but never helps anyone or, more importantly, does not use his wealth to lead others to Christ, then he has not lived a successful, fulfilling life. I'm not saying you have to go out on a street corner and preach. You can touch others by your life and actions alone. Everyone searches for happiness, and this happiness can be found, but it won't be found in wealth and prestige. It can be found only when we learn to enjoy all the gifts God has bestowed upon us. Look around. The world is a beautiful place and God is its greatest artist.

My sister-in-law, Theresa, whom I love and respect, suggested that I write this book. She asked me how I could always be happy and always have fun, regardless of the situation. I thought about what she said, and I realized that I honestly do enjoy every single day of my life. Whenever I am asked "How are you doing?" My response is "Great! Every day is a great day, some days are just better than others." There is a reason for that. I know that if I die today, I have lived a blessed and wonderful life. I have fulfilled my mission of teaching others, most importantly my family, about God and his Word. I am happy to have accomplished all that I have in the first fifty years of my life. I, like everyone else, have failed to live a perfect, sinless life. This is not something we need to dwell on, but to learn from and hopefully become a better person. The thing I am most proud of? It would not be the sales records, the basketball records, and not writing this book. It would be that I, along with my wife and our parents, have taught our children and grandchildren about the most important aspect of our lives. The ability to face adversity, trust God, and come back in a positive manner.

Is every day really a great day? I can honestly say yes! Do bad things happen to me? Of course they do. You have already read about a few of them. Some days I have good, bad, great, and awful events, all in the same day. There is no guarantee that anyone will ever have a good life. As an example, a book of the Bible follows the life of Job. Job lost everything he worked for. In our lives it would be comparable to losing your job, losing your spouse, your children dying, your reputation being ruined, and contracting a horrible disease, all through no fault of your own. It sure sounds like he had it a lot worse than any of us ever will. Through all of this, Job continued to believe in and serve God. God eventually rewarded Job after many years of suffering. We all have to learn from Job that while bad things do happen on a daily basis, it's the ability to trust God and come back that leads us to him for eternity.

The things that happen to you today, good, bad, great, or awful, will be forgotten fifty years from now. They will not matter. We may not even be here for another hour, so why fret and worry? It does no good. If you know that if you died today and are coming back to your Father, then go out and have a great day. You are on the right track for the greatest COMing BACK of all!

DEDICATION

First of all I want to thank my best friend, the Father, Son, and Holy Spirit, for my life, for strength, and for all my comebacks realized in the past and for those to come in the future. I also want to thank Him for the faith, direction, and thoughts he gave me as I wrote *Coming Back.*

I want to thank my wonderful wife, AnnaMarie Prebeg Coffey. She's an amazing wife and mother. She has stuck by me through the good times and the not so good. A big thanks for letting an old man live his dream and for the secret ice packs you provided after practice. Another thank you for introducing me to hiking so I'd quit playing basketball. Thank you last of all for being patient as I wrote *Coming Back.* I love you forever; you're the best!

A big thank you to my parents, C. E. Bud Coffey and Patricia Davis Coffey, better known as Patsy and Pop. They have always been there for me in every phase of my life, guiding me in the right direction while teaching me Chrisian values. Without them, many of my comebacks would not have been possible. I have learned many lessons from the stories of their own comebacks in life, and I bore witness to many of them myself. I hope they read *Coming Back* and are proud parents. I love you!

If not for my grandparents, Mama and Granddaddy Davis and Ma Bryte and Granddaddy Coffey, my life would be different in many ways. Through my stories you can see they played a large role in my life. I was very fortunate to have all four of my grandparents until I was thirty-five years old. I enjoyed every moment I spent with them. I enjoyed hearing every old story twenty or thirty times. I knew from their comeback stories that anything was possible. Working in a cotton mill in Rhodes Rhyne for five dollars a week was more than I could imagine. They were all good Christian people with good values. I think they would all be surprised to see their name in a book, and even more surprised I wrote it. I love and miss them all!

I have to give thanks to my children and grandchildren. Their presence has been the inspiration for many of our comebacks. All of them, in their early ages, have already faced tough situations they have had to come back from. I am most proud of them when the situation is negative but they remain positive and make the best of the situation. I thank each of them for the love and the happiness they have brought to our life. Our hope for them all is that they will love God, love one another, and come back strong throughout life.

Thanks to the best in-laws in the world, John and Filomina Prebeg. They are both wonderful and inspiring people. They have incredible comeback stories of their own that amaze me every time I hear them. If you think my coming back to play college basketball was something special, John pitched in an over–thirty-five baseball league at age seventy. What an inspiration. They are both deeply appreciated and loved. I also want to thank my sister-in-law Theresa Ferrell for suggesting I write again because I am "always happy." We love you very much!

I have to thank several coaches in my life. Thanks to Coach Larry Rhodes from Gastonia, North Carolina, the first real coach I ever had. He taught me the jab step and box out techniques that I still used at forty-six years of age. Thanks to East Lincoln coach Steve Cherry for keeping me on the straight and narrow as best he could. My biggest thank you to a coach goes to former Caldwell Community College coach Bill Payne. Without his support I could not have made my college basketball comeback or had a basis for writing *Coming Back*. Thank you, Coach Payne.

Another thank you goes out to my East Lincoln High School teammates from 1973–77. Thanks to all of you, many of my dreams came true. Without you it would not have been possible. A special thanks to Re-C Lowery for your friendship and for all those pinpoint passes you threw me.

I want to recognize all of my teachers from Asbury School, Iron Station School, Central Junior High, and East Lincoln High School. I just appreciate you putting up with me and teaching me all that you could.

I want to thank East Lincoln High School alumnus Barbara Murphy Jones for her early editing of *Coming Back* and for her friendship.

Thanks to professional tattoo artist Phillip Franklin for his initial ideas for the cover art work.

Thanks to all of these people, and others I failed to mention, for being a part of my life and for helping me along the comeback trails!